COLLABORATIVE PRACTICE IN THE BUILT ENVIRONMENT

EDITED BY TOM MUIR AND BRIAN RANCE
Faculty of the Built Environment, University of Central England,
Birmingham, UK

E & FN SPON
An Imprint of Chapman & Hall

London · Glasgow · Weinheim · New York · Tokyo · Melbourne · Madras

Published by E & FN Spon, an imprint of Chapman & Hall,
2–6 Boundary Row, London SE1 8HN, UK

Chapman & Hall, 2–6 Boundary Row, London SE1 8HN, UK

Blackie Academic & Professional, Wester Cleddens Road, Bishopbriggs,
Glasgow G64 2NZ, UK

Chapman & Hall GmbH, Pappelallee 3, 69469 Weinheim, Germany

Chapman & Hall USA, 115 Fifth Avenue, New York NY 10003, USA

Chapman & Hall Japan, ITP-Japan, Kyowa Building, 3F, 2-2-1 Hirakawacho,
Chiyoda-ku, Tokyo 102, Japan

Chapman & Hall Australia, 102 Dodds Street, South Melbourne, Victoria
3205, Australia

Chapman & Hall India, R. Seshadri, 32 Second Main Road, CIT East, Madras
600 035, India

First edition 1995

© 1995 E & FN Spon

Typeset in 10/12pt Caslon by Saxon Graphics Ltd, Derby

Printed in Great Britain by the Alden Press, Osney Mead, Oxford

ISBN 0 419 19560 2

A catalogue record for this book is available from the British Library

∞ Printed on permanent acid-free text paper, manufactured in accordance
with ANSI/NISO Z39.48-1992 and ANSI/NISO Z39.48-1984 (Permanence of
Paper).

CONTENTS

CONTRIBUTORS

Chris Arnison
Dean, School of Rural Economy,
Royal Agricultural College,
Cirencester, UK

Alan Cave
Director of Planning and
Consulting, Chesterton
International PLC, Birmingham,
UK

Richard Coles
Senior Lecturer, Faculty of the
Built Environment, University of
Central England, Birmingham, UK

Tony Collier
Dean of Faculty of the Built
Environment, University of
Central England, Birmingham,
UK

John Davison
Chief Executive, Groundwork
Foundation Ltd, Birmingham, UK

Maurice Ingram
Senior Lecturer, Faculty of the
Built Environment, University of
Central England, Birmingham,
UK

Patrick Loftman
Senior Lecturer, Faculty of the
Built Environment, University of
Central England, Birmingham, UK

Steve McCabe
Senior Lecturer, Faculty of the
Built Environment, University of
Central England, Birmingham, UK

Tom Muir
Head of Foundation Studies,
Faculty of the Built Environment,
University of Central England,
Birmingham, UK

Brian Rance
Head of Core Studies, Faculty of
the Built Environment, University
of Central England, Birmingham,
UK

David Shaw
Senior Lecturer, Department of
Civic Design, University of
Liverpool, UK

Richard Turkington
Senior Lecturer, Faculty of the
Built Environment, University of
Central England, Birmingham, UK

ABOUT THIS BOOK

This book explores issues relating to the organization and management of the construction and development industry. By a series of contributions from different authors, it seeks to demonstrate a variety of forces making for change in the industry. It identifies new and emergent collaborative practices in the built environment and the need for flexibility in the definition of professional roles.

Interwoven into the book are four underlying themes:

● Social, economic and political forces requiring a reappraisal of the organization and management of the development and construction industry.
● The need to reconsider traditional professional roles in the development process.
● A description and analysis of new and emergent forms of collaborative practice.
● The need for new forms of partnership in the development process.

Consequently, this book emphasizes new approaches to the organization and management of the development and construction industry. In particular it argues that the future effectiveness of the industry is dependent on a redefinition of professional roles. Instead of traditional specialist demarcation the book advocates an interprofessional team approach in order to respond to the current challenges and to look forward to the next century.

The book addresses issues that all aspiring built environment professionals need to know regardless of their future career specialisms. It is aimed primarily at first year undergraduate students on built environment courses which have set out to foster collaboration between different professional groupings. However, with many courses still closely tuned to traditional professional roles, we recognize that the book will have much wider relevance. It may well be of value to students in later years of their degrees as well as to pre-qualification education and training in some BTEC or general environmental courses.

The book has three broad objectives:

● To describe certain features of current practice.
● To analyse some of the major contextual changes affecting the industry.
● To point the way forward as to how the industry should respond to these challenges.

STRUCTURE

The book is in two sections. Chapters 1 to 5 seek to set the broad context of the forces shaping the industry and the fundamental challenges facing built environment professionals today. Chapters 6 to 10 contain case studies of emerging forms of collaborative practice.

● **Chapter 1** describes the process of professional specialization through history, reviews the organization and management of the industry and charts the changing nature of the building process and professional roles in it. The chapter provides a historical perspective and deals with different types of organization of the building project team, from traditional models through the interprofessional design practice to the package deal. It deals with professional attitudes towards interprofessional collaboration and the development of future collaborative practice.

● **Chapter 2** takes a more fundamental look at the nature of professionalism itself and advocates interprofessional approaches to decision making. It develops the rationale for greater collaboration between the professions in the future. It is argued that an understanding of the strengths and weaknesses of the concept of a profession is essential for the development of collaborative practice in the future.

● **Chapters 3 and 4** consider in more detail the organization of the industry. Chapter 3 deals with private practice and how different types of practice respond to the challenge of market competition. Chapter 4 looks at the rapidly changing role of the public sector in the development process as a context for the construction and development industry; it deals with the privatization of local authority roles and the effect of compulsory competitive tendering, the emergence of interagency government, the politicization of local government, the impact of European legislation and policy directives, and the emergence of new partnerships in the development process.

● **Chapter 5** recognizes the need for partnership between public and private sectors in the development process. It contains a description and advocacy of partnership arrangements and explains why the formation of effective partnership and collaborative team building are an essential element of modern practice. Using urban regeneration examples, it considers the importance of partnership arrangements in securing funding.

- **Chapter 6** considers in more detail the design/build approach to the construction process. It describes and compares the traditional and design/build methods of construction, the different stages of the process and client relationships, and advocates the need for change.

- **Chapter 7** considers the nature and relevance of project management approaches. It explains how and why the role of the project manager developed and identifies the relationship of the project manager with other parties in the construction process. It describes the management skills required and the contribution that can be made to developing multidisciplinary collaborative practice.

- **Chapter 8** is a series of examples of where different forms of community-based initiatives influence the nature of the development process. In considering how community involvement is seen as a key element in many agencies involved in the development process, it looks at the Groundwork Trust, Community Architecture, Planning Aid, Housing Action Trusts and City Challenge.

- **Chapter 9** places these considerations within a broader ecological context, by advocating the basic principles of sustainable development. It deals with the ecological principles underlying a concept of environmentalism and seeks to apply these concepts, offering an argument in support of sustainability as a philosophical basis for the development industry.

- **Chapter 10** summarizes the main themes of the book and points the way forward in terms of the future roles and organization of the built environment professions. It restates the importance of interprofessional collaborative practice for the future of the construction and development industry; it identifies the importance of education and training in preparing new professionals for this collaborative future in the twenty-first century and it draws comparisons with the organization of professions in continental Europe.

While all the chapters are interconnected, each can also be read as a chapter in its own right. Because of the range of material incorporated into this book, written as it is by a diverse range of specialist authors from education and practice, it can be used to gain an overview of the main issues facing the development and construction industry, or as a detailed reference on particular issues affecting the industry. All the authors have adopted the same format so that, while the style may vary, each chapter is organized into a common format and includes: theme, objectives, introduction, summary, checklist, workpieces, references and further reading.

The **workpieces** have been carefully thought out to enable students and teachers to benefit from either individual or group learning using common material. Most of the workpieces are designed to encourage discussion and develop skills in critical analysis as well as to promote the individual knowledge base of each reader and establish a spirit of broadly based enquiry for each reader.

INTRODUCTION TO COLLABORATIVE PRACTICE

CHAPTER ONE

TOM MUIR

What are the political and historical ideas which have helped to shape the organization of the professions we know today? How have the needs of society and clients of the built environment professions changed? What is the context for the rapid pace of change which we are experiencing today? Such questions are the starting points for this chapter, which revolves around historical evolution and change. It looks at the changes in client demands, technical performance specifications, materials, the social and economic structure of society and the professional responses to it within the development and construction industry.

It also develops the argument for increased collaboration between the professions and explores different ways in which this might be achieved.

After reading this chapter you should be able to:

- understand the origins of professional activity in the historical development of human society;

- understand how changing patterns of life styles and society values demand different professional services;

- identify the different technological changes in the development and construction industry in the twentieth century;

● recognize the advantages of offering an interprofessional service to the client and to the industry as a whole.

INTRODUCTION

It is an item of rare consensus amongst urban historians that of all humanity's great achievements, the city stands out as the greatest. As is inferred in the quotation below, the sum of its parts is exceeded in every way by the achievement of the whole:

> As the outer shell of the city grew, its interior likewise expanded: not merely its inner spaces, within the sacred precinct, but its inner life ... Activities that spring to life only on festal occasions in wider communities became part of the daily existence of the city. And what began as a wholesale transformation of the environment became a transformation of man.[1]

The earliest cities largely comprised huddled settlements whose only pretensions to a collective identity were through a few religious temples and external places of worship. Eventually the growth of trade necessitated the building of market places, walls and gates, with castles or palaces for the leaders. It is through the making and utilization of these communal facilities that the 'corporate' spirit and urbanity of the city developed.

A wide range of craft skills, a ready supply of materials, a large number of slaves and an intelligent, usually authoritarian upper class or priesthood were the ingredients for city growth and development in early times. Society also needed to focus on goals and objectives to work towards and an effective management framework to unify and direct people's efforts. This demanded efficient communications and the early recognition of the almost limitless potential of such collective behaviour.

This chapter is concerned with collaboration and collective endeavour with the common objective of creating the built environment. It identifies and traces the evolution of the construction process through history and charts the relative degree of independence sought by the main professions and trades involved.

HISTORY OF THE PROFESSIONS IN THE BUILT ENVIRONMENT

SPECIALIZATION OF HUMAN ACTIVITY

In the earliest settlements located in the Sumeria, Indus and Nile valleys, Burke[2] identifies the following conditions found to be necessary for successful communities:

● The provision of shelter and protection from wild beasts and human enemies.

- The capability to grow sufficient food to provide not only for everyday use but, in addition, to produce excesses for trade and to last until the next crop.
- The achievement of a division of labour enabling some members to specialize in making produce to exchange or trade. Later on such specialization resulted in them collaborating to build and develop the city.
- The capability to organize and participate in a system of bartering and trading.

It is in the division of labour that we can identify the antecedents of our present fragmented, multitrade, multiprofessional development and construction industry. After the early predominantly nomadic tribes, whose members lived, worked and aspired to provide everything that their immediate family required (Figure 1.1), came role specialization. Mumford[1] suggested that the specialized worker 'achieved excellence

Figure 1.1 Taos Pueblo, New Mexico, USA. Indians maintaining and repairing their adobe buildings in the same way as their ancestors had for hundreds of years.

and efficiency in the part to a degree impossible to reach except by such specialization: but he lost his grip on life as a whole'.

WORKPIECE 1.1

HISTORICAL DEVELOPMENT OF PROFESSIONAL SKILLS

Take your own professional skill and trace its origin through history, identifying the following stages:

- The earliest recognition of its use as a skill only.
- How it became incorporated as a specialism within a community.

- Adjustments which had to be made to an industrialized society.
- Professional incorporation.
- What role it has played in moves towards interprofessional collaboration.

THE DEVELOPMENT OF CRAFT AND TRADE ORGANIZATIONS

The identification of both a positive and a negative side to specialization is a recurring feature throughout the history and evolution of crafts, trades and professions in most industries, including the construction industry. Much later this 'enslavement' of the human spirit by requiring people to 'spend an entire life in a fractional occupation: the worker [being] a uniform replaceable part in a complex social machine'[1] was vividly characterized in the film *Metropolis* by Franz Laing. The specialized roles in the earliest urban settlements were extremely basic; however, their essential characteristic of being predominantly identified with the materials they used still held. Accordingly the main craft skills in the construction industries related to stonemasonry, woodworking, metal working, clay working and the making of burnt clay bricks. These manual craft skills needed to be augmented by those of the intellect when the communal buildings had to be designed and built. The project was required to satisfy a functional need in which its scale, form and structure all had to be appropriate and capable of being built using available technology and skills. This required an overall vision of the project at the outset.

Success in such a community was the prerogative of those committed to specialization and whose working life consisted of being integrated into a collective force within which much of their individuality had been subsumed. The role was formalized in ancient Egypt where craftsmen were restricted to conform, in perpetuity, to that function which was their hereditary role. Later in the writings of Plato in Periclean Greece, such principles were enshrined in intellectual dogma with his division of society into discrete classes, namely philosophers, warriors, craftsmen and husbandmen.

This overall trend, which followed through much of history, is again summed up by Mumford[1] who accurately foresaw precisely the situation in which we find ourselves today within the development and construction industry:

> Thus while the new urban form brought together and united a larger group of cooperating and interacting people than had ever existed in one place before, it also divided them into tightly separated strands, each deeply dyed in its occupational colours.

The Greeks and the Romans took city building into new dimensions. These encompassed new materials such as marble, cement, concrete and bronze; new social orders such as citizens, slaves, governors, senators; new sciences such as biology, mathematics, philosophy, physics; and finally, the skills required for many of our present traditional built environment professions – architecture, engineering and surveying.

This latter development gives us a key to future patterns of change in the division of labour and employment in the modern city. The social 'pyramid' in such cities placed the king or emperor at the top with priests, warriors and scribes at the next level down. Below them were merchants, craftsmen, peasants, sailors, house servants and freed men, with slaves being the lowest level of all.

EFFECTS OF CHANGING PATTERNS OF LIFE STYLES AND SOCIETY VALUES

The growth of the professions came about because the city had transcended its previously functional role and began to be seen by the new Greek intelligentsia as a manifestation of humanity's more cerebral aspirations.

THE GROWTH OF PROFESSIONAL SERVICES

> To know oneself ... is to know that one is not a disembodied mind or a walled-in city dweller but an integral part of an enveloping cosmos glimmering at last with self-consciousness.
> [*Phaedrus*, by Socrates]

The new professionals such as Ictinos (the architect and designer of the Parthenon), Hippodamus (the town planner of Miletus) and Meton the surveyor (a character in Aristophanes' play, *The Birds*) all testify to the transition from craftsman to creator.

With the Romans came engineering; the engineer created the vaults and arches which not only heralded a new technocracy but also provided visible evidence of a practical, scientifically based society. The stonemason became the dominant craftsman as his was the skill of handling the materials used for ceremonial buildings (Figure 1.2). Bricks

Figure 1.2 The Roman Coliseum, a vastly complex project from the points of view of design, planning and technology.

and mortar became the trade of the people and a new order was being established. The Roman city was much more of a city for all, and not simply (as in Greek cities) an expanse of primitive houses with inspired architectural achievements in creating temples, public buildings and communal facilities. The construction of paved and drained roads, tenements, theatres, etc. required the existence of an industry and, subsequently, a management system to ensure their continued usage. Road engineers, housing managers and building surveyors, although known by different names in ancient Rome, had an important role to play in the building and running of the Roman city. Mumford[1] recounts the remarkably modern commercial exploits of one Crassus who 'made a fabulous fortune in tenement house properties, boasted that he never spent money in building; it was more profitable to buy partly damaged old properties at fire sales and rent them with meagre repairs'.

Clearly the construction industry played an important role in the Roman town and the one kind of wheeled vehicle permitted by day in an otherwise pedestrianized Rome was that of the building contractor. Saalman[3] suggests that 'the entire mediaeval city was a market. Trade and production for trade went on in all parts of the city; in open spaces and closed spaces, public spaces and private spaces.'

The mediaeval city flourished under the feudal system and was financed by the burgeoning world trade that sprang from the opening of the New World and the Orient (both in the fifteenth century). The new cities with their castles, walls, gates and churches provided a stable platform for the restoration of a new social order not seen since the demise of the Roman empire. Although much of the Grecian philosophical perspective of cities and society had vanished, a new mercantile approach was born.

Initially the power in the city resided in the lord in the castle; however, towards the end of the Middle Ages the power had moved to the burghers and merchants with their grand, affluent houses grouped round the market squares. The crafts and trades of the construction industry established their guilds which 'secured, for the artisan as well as the merchant, not only freedom, but an unprecedented economic status'.[4] They also regulated production and controlled standards of workmanship of their members, thereby establishing themselves as protectors of the public interest and developing a role which gave them status and prestige in the city.

The guilds originated in Anglo-Saxon times, when the concepts of fellowship, common faith and common work were pillars of society. The guilds grew from religious fraternities and subsequently developed somewhat unusual characteristics such as those found in the Order of Freemasons or the English Friendly Society.

One of the prime achievements of the guilds was to protect the interests of their members and to defend their 'employment territory'. This they did most effectively. However, Mumford's[1] concern over the inevitable segregation that this would cause between the different guilds, even those within the building crafts and trades, was justified.

The mediaeval master mason combined the functions of architect, builder and clerk of works but had to understand masonry more than any other craft. A mediaeval building of almost any size comprised 75% masonry, the remainder being carpentry, joinery, plumbing and glazing. Even such things as the design of a vault, buttress or foundation, which we would now consider to be engineering concepts, were in the mason's province.

In terms of education, Lethaby[5] described it thus:

Mastership was closely parallel to that of a Master of Arts in the university, that is, Guild of Letters. By serving a seven year apprenticeship he became a Bachelor or Companion, and, on presenting a proper work thesis, he was admitted Master.

CHANGES IN THE MIDDLE AGES

This 'craft apprenticeship' route was in contrast to the 'inspired amateur or learned gentleman' who dabbled in architecture as part of his leisure activities. In between these two were many more prosaic architects who plied their profession in the service of doctrinaire orders and 'made architecture an affair of rules'.[6]

Few of the other roles that we associate with the building team had evolved as yet. There was, however, a 'treasurer' or 'surveyor' who backed up the architect and dealt with matters of finance and was to all intents an employer or client.

DEVELOPMENTS OF THE EIGHTEENTH AND NINETEENTH CENTURIES

By the end of the eighteenth century and the beginning of the nineteenth, a more complex and sophisticated society provided the incentive for developments such as those in London's Regent Street and in Bath. Perhaps Bath (Figure 1.3) offers us the best example where cooperative ventures between, in this case, the Prince Regent, Beau Nash and the architects – the Woods (father and son) – resulted in the dramatic redevelopments of the Crescent and Circus.

This was speculative development which succeeded in terms of planning, architecture and financing and, as with other developments such as those in Bloomsbury, Mayfair and Belgravia in London, set the tone for urbane city living in eighteenth century Britain. It also estab-

Figure 1.3 Royal Crescent, Bath.

lished the skills which ultimately resulted in the property development explosions of the nineteenth and twentieth centuries and generated the complementary skills of estate management.

The latter profession was already becoming established. It grew out of the management needs of the great country estates initially owned by the landed gentry, but increasingly becoming the property of the new wealthy industrialists who preferred to leave the cities (despoiled by their factories) and emulate their aristocratic predecessors. It was in these estates that another great traditional partnership emerged – that of the owner, the architect and the landscape architect. Building on the experience of earlier partnerships involving people such as Nash, Adam and Capability Brown, the late nineteenth century Lutyens and Gertrude Jekyll make a profound turn-of-the-century contribution to the English landscape while at the same time acquiring increasing recognition for their respective professions.

So where do our professions stand as we enter the modern era? The architects, having resolved their dilemma between the craft base or the dilettante amateur chose the middle route of professional competence and, by 1865, had established a separate professional body called the Royal Institute of British Architects (RIBA) to protect their name and role.

The Royal Institution of Chartered Surveyors was also established in the mid nineteenth century, along with the Institute of Civil Engineers. Both of these were to be subdivided in order to promote their individual professional identities and to protect and promote their skills – precisely the reasons which prompted the original professional bodies to establish themselves in the first place. (Chapter 2 refers to the process of professionalism.)

It was self-evident during the nineteenth century and into the twentieth that the construction industry, in line with manufacturing processes, was becoming increasingly complex. No one profession or craft could exercise the same influence as the master masons had done in earlier times. Clearly there was a need for the workforce to come to terms with and master the new materials and techniques of design and assembly.

The division of labour that developed in the early city had now evolved to an advanced level. A fundamental division was arising between the professions and the crafts (now becoming trades) with the professions being removed off-site and grouped in 'practices', and trades

ENTERING THE MODERN ERA

9

remaining on site. New building techniques resulted in the addition of two new members to the construction team: the manufacturer and the supplier. These reflected the almost universal practice of manufacturing components in a factory, often many miles from the site, and then distributing them through suppliers to the place of their assembly.

Large buildings are now seen not so much as monolithic constructions but more as static mechanisms comprising a series of distinctly different yet totally interactive systems:

- structural – the element which holds the building up and retains its rigidity;
- cladding – which maintains the weatherproofing qualities of the building;
- services – environmental control systems such as air-conditioning, water, gas, electricity (often this is highly complex in a modern building and can consume up to 60% of the total cost).

Perhaps the growth of specialization is the single change in society most relevant to the subject of this chapter and indeed this book. Specialization of roles and skills resulted inevitably in interdependency and thus created the growth of communities, with people becoming increasingly reliant on each other for the provision and maintenance of their total environment. From this development can be seen the expectation of our modern society which is that each person will acquire a specific skill that can only be ultimately productive when used in conjunction with other skills.

Each of the built environment professions referred to throughout this book can be seen to have evolved through this process. That evolution has not yet finished and this chapter will explore how the professions, having evolved into individual separate commercial practices, are now readjusting once more to a changing context in which cooperation and team work are required for success.

RECENT CHANGES INFLUENCING THE CONSTRUCTION AND DEVELOPMENT INDUSTRY

Until the Second World War, the construction and development industry in the UK had changed little for centuries. Although new materials were being employed, their use had been absorbed into the traditional practices of the industry and they were still seen as direct replacements for the traditional materials. It was only in the latter part of this century that a gradual realization of other factors, caused partly by social and economic changes as a result of the war, produced major new policies and programmes. The following are some of these main changes:

- Major rebuilding programme targeted at the bombed out centres of cities.
- Massive new public housing developments both at the edge and in the inner areas of our cities.
- Political pressure for great speed in carrying out these programmes, including subsidies.
- Introduction of prefabrication procedures into the building industry after their success in the munitions factories during wartime.
- Use of female labour force causing a revolution both at work and in the home.
- Setting up of a planning system to manage, control and stimulate these development programmes.

Even with all of this, the construction industry was slow to respond. Only in the early 1960s was it realized that this traditional structure of small, separate professional units, operating independently both of each other and of the construction process, was inefficient. It was also seen as being incapable of responding to the needs of new types of clients.

TRADITIONAL ORGANIZATION OF THE CONSTRUCTION AND DEVELOPMENT INDUSTRY

The essential characteristic of every construction project was the 'discrete' nature of the 'actors'. Each professional was in a separate office being appointed by, and sometimes directly responsible to, the architect (the traditional leader of the design team) and in some cases directly responsible to the client. Lines of communication tended to be convergent and did not always allow for the most efficient use of time.

This system more accurately reflected the traditionally independent structure of the professions rather than the needs of a rapidly changing industry. The nature of professionalism and the professions is discussed in the next chapter; however, the model was usually one of a smallish office comprising possibly four to ten staff from the same professional background giving a single professional service to each project.

CHANGING PATTERN SINCE THE 1950s

To give a clearer understanding of the changing pattern of the construction 'team' it would be best to explore the evolving roles of the other main participants, namely the client, the professional services and the contractor.

CHANGING ROLE OF THE CLIENT Increasingly sophisticated management structures have characterized the typical large corporate client of the last 20 years. Complex systems of internal cost control and budgetary management have resulted in a preference for

STRUCTURE OF A PROFESSIONAL OFFICE

The diag... ...es what a typical management structure of a professional office might be. It could be an architect, quantity surveyor, ...ngineer (civil, mechanical, electrical or services) or any other in the construction industry.

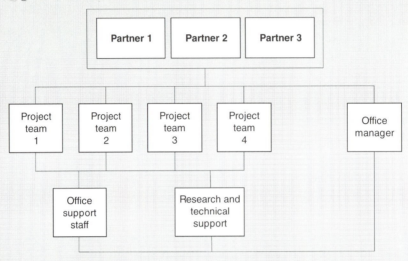

Typical management structure of a professional office.

Using this as a model, carry out the following tasks:

1. Draw a similar chart for an office whose management structure you are familiar with.
2. Indicate by means of smaller 'scale' diagrams how the clients, consultants and contractors relate to the office structure you have drawn.

dealing with a similarly structured organization when involved in the building and development process. These clients have little wish to have direct and exclusive contractual relationships with, say, the architect, quantity surveyor, structural engineer, interior designer, or even the building contractor. Preference has been indicated for single project managers who would coordinate and manage all parts of the process – both design and construction – providing the client with one single point of contact for the whole project.

CHANGING ROLE OF PROFESSIONAL SERVICES

Most of the professional institutions in the construction and development industry have strong and individualistic backgrounds and are proud of their 'separateness'. The RIBA, RICS and ICE were all set up in the nineteenth century and, as shown earlier, their historic nature has traditionally directed them into single profession practices.

In the 1950s and 1960s, however, some large architectural practices such as the Building Design Partnership, and Robert Matthew–Johnson–Marshall and Partners (now RMJM Ltd) recognized the change in clients' requirements and started to broaden their practice to offer surveying, structural and building services engineering in addition to the original architectural design. The development of multiprofessional design teams allowed practices to carry out a much wider range and scale of project while offering the client the clearer, simplified management structure which was increasingly demanded. Another factor which influenced this move was the growing use of prefabrication and system building methods. This required a level of corporate planning and management that transcended barriers and more or less forced the establishment of a tightly programmed, professionally integrated process within a clear, centralized management structure.

Quantity surveyors found that their skills as the 'accountants' of the industry were particularly appropriate to the new money-conscious corporate client. Several large practices have become increasingly involved in construction project management where they offer a management driven, cost-conscious leadership to the building teams. This has proved to be very attractive to large clients such as local authorities and banks.

CHANGING ROLE OF THE CONTRACTOR The large construction firms recognized that, whereas the professional consultants could certainly provide a corporate or interprofessional design process, only they had the capability to deliver the entire product. The first such ventures were known as 'package deals' in which the contractor acted as the project coordinator, employing all professionals, consultants and subcontractors required to carry out the project. The attraction for the client in this process was the ability to delegate the responsibility for the whole project, from inception to completion, to the member of the team whose role it was to construct the building. This process was one which many clients feared was most vulnerable to loss of cost control, and so it seemed sensible to give budgeting responsibility to the 'package deal' contractor as well.

In the 1950s and 1960s, this proved a most popular option and in Birmingham the major redevelopment of the city centre was carried out using competition between 'package deal' contractors. They competed on broad project briefs prepared by the local authority, with contractors appointing chartered surveyors to prepare a development brief based upon maximum earning capacity of the site within the local authority's

WORKPIECE 1.3

THE BUILDING PROCESS

The diagram illustrates in a much simplified form how a project is carried out using traditional on-site building methods. The project is a small *in situ* concrete building from excavation to roofing.

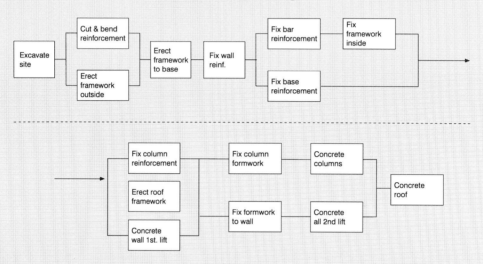

Traditional building process.

From studying this sequence diagram and from what you know about construction practice, draw a similar chart showing how a similar building might be erected, only this time using a prefabricated system with components fabricated off-site and brought on-site for assembly.

brief and with their architects drawing the design within a cost plan prepared by quantity surveyors.

CHANGES IN BUILDING METHODS   Prefabricated system building methods were particularly appropriate for the 'package deal' as the contractor/builder was, by necessity, heavily involved in the development of the system itself, and therefore exerted a strong influence in any design process using that system.

A particularly complex example of this occurred in the 1960s in Thamesmead, where the contractor located the factory making the components of the building system used in many of the homes within the Thamesmead New Town zoned area. Therefore much of the labour force in the new town was dependent on the continued success of Thamesmead for both their home and their job. This example highlights the level of interconnection which can be created within the prefabrication system. In this case it bound the designers, the Development Corporation, the construction (manufacturing) company and the workforce into a network of mutual dependency.

The general move to more collaboration between members of the development and building industry team has produced differing responses from the various professions.

ARCHITECTS   Collaboration has been seen by many architects as the greatest single threat to their long established position as the natural 'leader' of the team. The view is often expressed that designers must provide leadership and that if they do not the quality of the building, in both functional and aesthetic terms, will suffer. The weaknesses in this argument were provided by a plethora of studies which suggested that the traditional method of independent practice was equally susceptible to considerable criticism for inadequate performance of buildings, not only in functional and aesthetic terms but also in technical, management and cost control aspects.

QUANTITY SURVEYORS   Quantity surveyors, whose roles include cost planning, budgetary monitoring and preparation of bills of quantities, have found a new, more effective role in collaborative practices. They now often see themselves as the new natural leader of the building team in which effective management and budgetary controls are felt, by the client, to be of paramount importance.

ENGINEERS (SERVICES, STRUCTURAL, ELECTRICAL)
Engineers are involved with only part of a project, i.e. the structure or the services (such as air-conditioning). Therefore they have always seen themselves as part of a team, except when the project is a large civil engineering one such as a dam or road. Nevertheless most engineers welcome a closer link with the other professionals in the design team, as closer communication allows for a quicker and more appropriate response to change. It can also be an opportunity for the engineer to make a more positive contribution to the design process.

LANDSCAPE ARCHITECTS AND INTERIOR DESIGNERS   These professionals often feel like the Cinderellas of the team, brought in to correct the faults created by others. Collaboration at an early stage, if not right from the outset, is seen as a positive opportunity for

PROFESSIONAL ATTITUDES TO INTERPROFESSIONAL COLLABORATION

landscape architects and interior designers to make an influential contribution to the final overall design.

DEVELOPERS/ESTATE MANAGERS   These roles are now open to a wider range of people. Within the last 10 years, architects have been released from their professional restriction and may now participate in the development process commercially. Possibly some of the most exciting developments have come from combining the commercial acumen of the property developer with the imagination of the designer and applying it to some of our major urban problems.

TOWN PLANNERS   Planners are not often seen as members of the design/development team, yet it is the planner who often has a key role to play when partnership ventures occur between local authorities and the private sector. Within a true interprofessional collaborative venture, the planner can work with the team to realize planning objectives rather than being regarded as an external constraint to free market enterprise. The public sector rarely has the resources to implement plans, therefore such collaboration could be seen as an attractive way to influence and stimulate development in a positive way.

THE NATURE OF INTERPROFESSIONAL COLLABORATION OBJECTIVES OF INTERPROFESSIONAL COLLABORATION

What are the objectives of interprofessional collaboration? What does it achieve and why is it better than previous models?

These objectives might be:

1.   To break down stereotyped attitudes.
2.   To improve the flow of information.
3.   To improve the decision-making process.
4.   To avoid abortive work through duplication.
5.   To increase cost effectiveness of design procedures.

BREAKING DOWN STEREOTYPED ATTITUDES   It does not take long for new recruits to the professions to acquire a complete 'kit' of stereotyped views about their fellow professionals – the sports-car driving architect with bow tie who cares only for the aesthetics; the long-coated, homburg hatted developer who sees only profit in a development; the 'hardhat' engineer lost in calculations, etc. These caricatures may be amusing, but the attitudes they reflect run deep within the industry and are divisive. They inhibit honest communication and

FORMS OF PROFESSIONAL PRACTICE

Professional practices can combine or share their professional services in a project in a variety of different ways. Make a list of as many as you can think of and analyse each using the following criteria (the diagrams illustrate some examples):

1. How much genuine collaboration can be carried out.
2. What contribution to the project each type of combination can make so that the sum is greater than its parts.
3. How collaboration is achieved between the different professions.
4. What increased potential the system of sharing can make to the practice.

The list of different groupings should be illustrated by diagrammatic sketches linking the participants appropriately.

Week	1	2	3	4	5	6	7	8	9	10	11	12	13	14	15	16	17
B.S.						Building regulations approval											
Q.S.		Cost Plan 1	Cost Plan 2							Bill of quantities							
Arch.		Brief analysis and sketch des.		Submit for plan. appl'n						Production drawing							
Struct. Eng.				Consult on drgs.						Struct. cals. and drgs.							
Mech. Eng.										Service drgs. + calc. prop.							
Town Plan.				Consult for plan.		Evaluate plans for planning approval											
L'scape		Cons. on des.								L'scape drgs.							
Contr.													Tenders prep.			Const. start.	

Consortium Association
Client approaches anyone
who then brings in others

Consortium Partnership
Client approaches the
Partnership.

often mask ignorance, thereby denying the logical resolution of complex problems that require genuine collaboration to solve.

IMPROVING INFORMATION FLOW   The essence of collaboration is communication. Effective decision making is the product of good communications and hence collaboration is the catalyst for good project management. It helps in both the setting and the achieving of mutually agreed goals, and in the monitoring of the procedures set up to achieve them.

IMPROVING THE DECISION-MAKING PROCESS   As well as having enough information, it is the range and quality of information available when required that contribute to good, effective decision making. Interprofessional collaboration can seek to achieve this in two ways:

● By indicating, through education and experience, an awareness of other professional values and procedures. It is hoped that this will result in a greater acknowledgement of the contribution they might make to individual decisions.

● By providing an opportunity through proximity or user friendly media for quality contact between project partners.

AVOIDING ABORTIVE WORK THROUGH DUPLICATION
Good management requires an economy and efficiency of procedures geared to developing a situation and taking it forward from its previous position. Duplication occurs when cooperation breaks down and separate, parallel procedures are being implemented by people who are unaware of each other's activities. Collaboration is designed to eliminate such waste and to ensure that a project follows a continuous sequential development process.

INCREASING THE COST EFFECTIVENESS OF DESIGN PROCEDURES   By achieving the first four objectives, it should be expected that substantial economies in time will be achieved without any loss in quality. Indeed a gain in quality due to an increase in the amount and quality of the information available could be expected.

OPERATIONAL EXPERIENCES

In situations where interprofessional teams have been operating, certain experiences have been identified. They represent only some of the many conditions under which collaborative teams work and serve to offer some initial assessments.

LEADERSHIP   In a situation in which project teams were set up without clearly establishing a leader, the role of leader tended to be acquired by the team member who most quickly identified with the goals and objectives of the project and whose ideas for developing it won most respect from the others. Rarely did any one profession consistently supply group leaders and as the teams were composed mostly of architects, engineers (structural and services) and quantity surveyors, this would certainly contradict one commonly held rubric!

STRESS   Where teams of mixed professionals worked on particular projects intensively for some time, the stress levels on some members of the team seemed to be higher than would have been predicted in more traditionally constituted situations. This could be the result of several factors:

● The inability to hide behind conventional professional wisdoms when constantly challenged and driven by a highly motivated team.

● The lack of education in interprofessional skills leaving the young professional ill equipped for such an intensive process.

● The competitive nature of the team where ideas and progress paid little or no attention to conventional roles and concentrated almost entirely on performance.

WORKLOAD   The contribution of different professional skills to a project varies from profession to profession. Architects are involved from inception to completion. Quantity surveyors have early involvement at the cost planning stage and then intensively during preparation of the Bill of Quantities. This variation of optimum workload by profession and project requires careful planning and managing in order to achieve a balanced workload across an office team. Experience gained from some offices which operate in this way suggest that additional specialist consultancy might prove necessary to ensure that the desired balance of workload is achieved.

WORKPIECE 1.5

NEW CONCEPTS OF TEAM WORKING

Collaboration between different professionals requires the introduction of new working methods incorporating new concepts of team working. It also requires changes in attitudes in order to break down some of the traditional stereotypes each profession has of the others.

List what you feel are the main changes required to achieve effective collaboration. List them under:

● new working methods;
● changes in attitude.

There is no guarantee that collaboration will result from simply creating multiprofessional proximity. Collaboration requires a set of conditions which create the climate for information 'networking' and collective identification with common problems. A fundamental state of mind which underpins genuine collaboration is a recognition that leadership

THE COLLABORATIVE PROCESS

may rotate from team member to team member, depending upon the prevailing demands at any one time.

This process is as important at corporate level as it is at individual level and such 'conditions' required might include:

- A clear management framework which recognizes the essential needs of effective interprofessional collaboration.
- An open-minded approach to both problem identification and problem solving.
- A degree of 'lateral thinking' so that the advantages of having a multiprofessional team can be exploited by approaching problems from unexpected directions.
- Recognition that the project holds primacy over other goals or objectives and that success in the project is the goal for all professional contributors.
- Acknowledgement that the management goal for interprofessional collaboration is to ensure that each participant pushes the others in a collaborative striving for a common achievement, namely the project.
- Not allowing professional restrictive practices to inhibit the true spirit of collaboration within the project.

WORKPIECE 1.6

STRUCTURE OF A MULTIPROFESSIONAL OFFICE

Prepare a hypothetical practice structure for a multiprofessional office incorporating the 'balance' of different professional skills which you think capable of offering the best service to both client and contractor while still having economic and professional viability in its own right.

Describe how you would structure such a practice so as to ensure that each project undertaken exploited fully the multidisciplinary nature of the staff.

Possible groupings:

- office structure;
- design teams – multiple project;
- single-project teams.

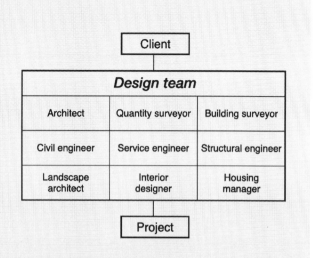

Structure of a multiprofessional office

The move towards a wider use of interprofessional collaborative procedures is now well established. Few large-scale projects nowadays are carried out in the traditional manner and there are as many new and innovative project management structures as there are projects. A recent development is the growth of international consortia such as the one which carried out the project at Canary Wharf (Figure 1.4) in London's Docklands where a multinational team comprising Canadian developers, American architects and the Docklands Development Corporation combined in a complex collaborative venture.

NEW DEVELOPMENTS

Figure 1.4 Canary Wharf, London Docklands, an example of the scale and complexity of a modern development project.

Broadgate (Figure 1.5) in the City of London is another example. The initial team was lead by Ove Arup but was eventually replaced by the developers, who brought in the American firm, Skidmore Owings and Merrill, as coordinating architects.

Figure 1.5 Broadgate, City of London, a large project involving a high proportion of foreign consultants and suppliers.

In both cases, the overall managing and programming of the project was carried out by overseas professionals using (in the case of Canary Wharf) foreign developers and (in the case of Broadgate) German suppliers and fitters of cladding. Canary Wharf had a substantial link with the public sector through the Docklands Development Corporation and London Underground by way of the Docklands Light Railway (DLR).

These immensely complex projects consistently demanded both advanced levels of collaboration across national as well as professional boundaries and greater levels of management and programming skills than had previously been required of the built environment professions.

NEW SKILLS

Professional competence must now be defined as incorporating skills other than those traditionally associated with any one profession. Management is now an essential component of professional practice and is relevant across all professional boundaries. Effective management demands not only the skills to manage but also the (often underrated) work in which all members of the team suppress individual professional agendas in order to solve, collectively, problems posed by the project.

Interpersonal skills will be required to accept changes in team leadership and to minimize problems of misplaced positions being taken up by team members based upon traditional roles and perceived status.

Competence, relevance, decisiveness, approachability, fairness and efficiency are some of the qualities which generate leadership potential. The demands of relevance will inevitably result in leadership changing when and where it seems most natural for it to do so.

International competition is undoubtedly going to be fundamental to the success of British industry in the twenty-first century. The European Union ensures open access to tendering across all borders of its member states, and if the construction and development industry in this country fails to organize itself to compete effectively, it will fail to receive major contracts even in the UK. This has already happened in the examples of Broadgate and Canary Wharf.

Research carried out as early as 1965[7] showed that group interprofessional consortia were being developed in Europe and that there was a strong realization that such developments were essential if Europe was to survive the aggressive and, in management and marketing terms, sophisticated competition from America.

FUTURE PROBLEMS OF PRACTICE

This chapter traces the origins of professions in the specialization of human activity through the ages. This historical perspective charts the development of craft and trade organizations from the earliest civilizations through to the growth of professional bodies in more recent times. The advantages and disadvantages of the traditional highly specialized organization of the development and construction industry is discussed and the development of more collaborative approaches is considered and promoted. Many of the issues raised in this introductory chapter are considered in more detail in later chapters.

SUMMARY

The issues covered in this chapter are:

- specialization of human activity;
- the development of craft and trade organizations;
- effects of changing patterns of life styles and society values;
- the growth of changes in the Middle Ages;
- development in the eighteenth and nineteenth centuries;
- recent changes influencing the construction and development industry;
- the traditional organization of the construction and development industry;
- the changing role of the client;
- the changing role of professional services;

CHECKLIST

● the changing role of the contractor;
● professional attitudes to interprofessional collaboration;
● the collaborative process.

REFERENCES

1. Mumford, L. (1986) *The City in History*, Pelican.
2. Burke, G. (1971) *Towns in the Making*, Edward Arnold, London.
3. Saalman, H. (1968) *Mediaeval Cities*, Studio Vista, London.
4. Childe, G. (1942) *What Happened in History*, Pelican.
5. Lethaby, W.R. (1974) *Architecture, Mysticism and Myth*, 2nd edn, Architectural Press, London.
6. Briggs, M.S. (1925) *A Short History of the Building Crafts*, Clarendon Press, Oxford.
7. RIBA (1965) *Guide to Group Practice and Consortia*, Royal Institute of British Architects, London.

FURTHER READING

Cherry, G.E. (1931) *Cities and Plans, the Shaping of Urban Britain in the Nineteenth and Twentieth Centuries*, Edward Arnold, London.
Law, E.H. (1961) *What is History?*, Pelican.
Lethaby, W.R. (1956) *Architecture, Nature and Magic*, Duckworth, London.
Morris, A.E.J. (1979) *History of Urban Form*, Longman.
Sprott, W. (1962) *Human Groups*, Penguin.

PROFESSIONALISM IN THE BUILT ENVIRONMENT

BRIAN RANCE

One of the main factors affecting the nature of collaborative practice between professional groups in the built environment is the value assumptions that professionals hold. These value systems largely determine the ways in which professionals see their role and the contribution other professional groups can make to the construction and development process. Value systems can be described as a complex set of attitudes and beliefs which determine the manner in which professionals define their role and respond to the role definitions of other professional groups. Using workpieces and examples this chapter seeks to explore these value systems. It aims to encourage students to question traditional role definitions and promote interprofessional approaches to collaborative practice.

After reading this chapter you should be able to:

- understand that the concept of a profession is complex and problematical;

- be aware of the limitations and contradictions of the concept of a professional and be prepared to undertake further study;

- understand the process of professionalization and its effect on collaborative practice in the development and construction industry.

INTRODUCTION

The nature of collaborative practice and the historical development of the professions in the construction and development industry have been explored in Chapter 1. A central feature of current practice is the complex relationships between many professional groups. In order to explore these relationships in more detail, it is necessary to define and critically analyse the meaning of the term 'professional' and to consider the concept of professionalism.

The extent to which different professional groups actually collaborate in practice depends on:

● the nature of the task;
● professional role definitions;
● the institutional context.

The nature of the task will determine the precise grouping of professional skills required and Chapter 1 of this book describes the emergence of modern interdisciplinary collaborative practice as a response to the increasing complexity of the industry.

Professional role definitions determine what are considered to be appropriate areas of concern or interest for particular professional groups. They also act to establish accepted professional boundaries and demarcation of activities and responsibilities for the task. These role definitions are often deeply rooted and honed by custom and practice. They are nurtured by a subtle process of socialization through education and training.

Collaboration between professional groups differs according to the constraints and opportunities provided by the institutional context. For example, the practices common in the private sector (Chapter 3) are different from the practices in the public sector (Chapter 4).

This chapter is concerned with the definition of professional roles within the opportunities and limitations of the concept of professionalism itself, leading to an evaluation of the interdisciplinary nature of the task.

WHAT IS A PROFESSION?

Millerson[1] gives a working definition of a profession:

A type of higher grade non-manual occupation with both subjectively and objectively recognized status, possessing a well defined area of study or concern and providing a definite service after advanced education and training.

From this working definition the following aspects will be considered in more detail:

- When is an occupation regarded as a profession?
- Does a profession have a well defined area of study or concern?
- What is the role of education and training?

In addition the following issues will be considered:

- The desire for professional autonomy.
- The desire for altruistic service.
- The desire to present professional activity as a technical/value neutral matter.

There are two basic ways of classifying professions: the traditional 'trait' approach and a 'functionalist' approach.

The **trait approach** seeks to identify the common attributes of a profession; that is, the more professional traits an occupation has, the more likely it is to be regarded as a profession.

WHEN IS AN OCCUPATION REGARDED AS A PROFESSION?

WORKPIECE 2.1

THE 'TRAITS' OF PROFESSIONALISM

List a number of professions which you may be familiar with and consider to what extent the following traits apply:

- Restricted entry
- Qualification by education and training
- Definite body of theoretical knowledge
- Professional institution
- High status/appropriate remuneration
- Code of conduct
- Clear view of client
- Commitment to service
- Acts in the 'public interest'
- Objectivity and value neutrality
- Commitment to continued professional development

WORKPIECE 2.2

GENERALIST/SPECIALIST PROFESSIONS

How do built environment professionals measure up? Rank the following professions according to the degree of professionalism. Can you think of any other professions in the built environment? Do you think this classification of generalist and specialist professions is appropriate?

Generalist	Specialist	
architects	urban designers	housing managers
engineers	landscape architects	development controllers
surveyors	building surveyors	project managers
planners	quantity surveyors	highway engineers
managers	estate managers	civil engineers
		structural engineers

The alternative way of classifying professions is referred to as the **functionalist approach**, which examines the role that professions play in society.

Johnson[2] sees professionals as mediating in a producer/consumer relationship. In the built environment the producer may be regarded as the developer/builder and the consumer as the client/public. For example, the planning profession may be seen as mediating between the developer and the community – that is, facilitating development in a manner that protects and enhances the interest of the community. A functionalist view directs attention to:

● the initiators of the development process;
● the client or consumer of any developments;
● the role played by professionals in managing this process.

WORKPIECE 2.3

'FUNCTIONALIST' VIEWS OF PROFESSIONS

List a number of professions with which you may be familiar (see the list in Workpiece 2.2) and consider who is the producer and who is the consumer in relation to any professional role. Refer to the examples suggested in the text in the section 'What is a profession?'. Consider each professional role as a mediator between a producer/initiator and a consumer/client, and use the pro forma to help complete this exercise.

Producer/initiator   Profession   Consumer/client

DOES A PROFESSIONAL HAVE A WELL DEFINED AREA OF INTEREST?

Millerson's[1] definition implies that a profession must have a definite area of study or concern. A traditional view of a profession will highlight the specialist technical expertise of practitioners. According to this view it is a contradiction in terms to have a generalist profession or for practitioners to be technical experts in a wide field of activity. Therefore professions are:

● inherently specialist in nature;
● demonstrating expertise in a limited field of knowledge;
● likely to champion a technical interpretation of the field.

These issues can be illustrated by an exercise which seeks to identify the 'core' areas of professional activity and what it is that gives a profession any claim to specialist expertise.

THE 'CORE' AREA OF PROFESSIONAL ACTIVITY

Referring to the diagram, analyse several professions that you are particularly interested in by discussing and defining:

(A) the core area of professional activity;
(B) the area of activity commonly associated with the profession but not regarded as a core activity;
(C) the area of activity which you feel should be commonly associated with the profession.

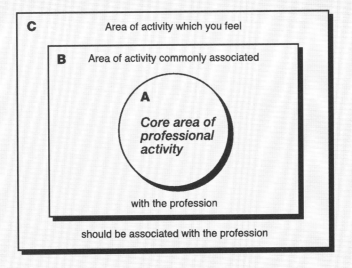

C Area of activity which you feel

B Area of activity commonly associated

A

Core area of
professional
activity

with the profession

should be associated with the profession

A profession goes through a process of professionalization which involves the following features:

● expansion to establish the boundaries of professional activity;
● establishing autonomy and monopoly over a particular field of knowledge and activity involving the recognition of specific skills and abilities;
● acquiring social status.

Within the expansionist logic of the growth and establishment of professions there is the danger that the specialist technical expertise identified above as central to the concept of a profession may be lost or diluted.

According to the logic of professionalization, there are two probabilities as professions succeed and manage to grow:

● They incorporate a new area of activity not previously associated with a profession. For example, the planning profession has shown a remarkable ability to colonize related areas such as economic development.

● They establish a monopoly over a wider area of concern, often involving encroachment across professional boundaries. A good example here is the current demarcation disputes between architects, building surveyors, quantity surveyors and building engineers in the construction industry.

Established professions are likely to subdivide into new professional groupings where the specialist nature of the activity is easier to recognize. Laffin[3] has described the process of professionalization in relation to the development of highway engineering and housing management.

WORKPIECE 2.5

THE PROCESS OF PROFESSIONALIZATION

Take a profession that you are particularly interested in and research its origins in relation to the concept of professionalization. Consider the following questions as part of this exercise:

● When was the profession first formed?

● What was the original impetus for its formation?
● Did the profession grow out of another profession?
● Did government legislation figure significantly in the origins of the profession?
● What are the major stages in the evolution of the profession?

WHAT IS THE ROLE OF EDUCATION AND TRAINING?

One of the characteristics associated with professionalism is that entry to the profession is determined by the acquisition of approved qualifications. Professional education is concerned with:

● the acquisition of a body of theoretical knowledge;
● the acquisition of skills, expertise and judgement;
● the adoption of a set of professional values and commitment.

Part of the claim to professionalism is based upon the acquisition of an exclusive body of theoretical knowledge, which involves an understanding of complex phenomena and processes. To take an example from another field: medical doctors are regarded as professionals because they are presumed to have theoretical knowledge about the workings of the human body – knowledge which is not generally available to the layman without advanced training and education. Similarly in the built environment an architect is presumed to be in possession of the skills, knowledge and imagination to create aesthetic and effective built forms.

In some professions in the built environment a distinction is made between professionals and technicians. This appears to be particularly true in the more design-based professions which may require a greater degree of creativity and imagination such as architecture, landscape architecture and town planning. In Workpiece 2.4, it may be helpful to consider how technical the core area of activity is and whether technicians can cover these activities. Within some professions there are demarcation disputes between professionals and technicians since technicians appear to be able to perform many of the tasks accorded to professionals. If there is a distinction between the roles of technician and professional it seems to relate primarily to:

- different education and training;
- the use of judgement where technical solutions are not available;
- perceived status.

Thus not only are professionals required to have a sound basis of theoretical knowledge and understanding of their particular field, but they are also required to tackle practical problems and manage complex processes in a way that demonstrates skill, expertise and judgement. These aspects of professional behaviour are closely related to the adoption of a set of professional values, comprising a set of ideals, attitudes and roles, which determine how a professional will behave in any given situation.

The content of professionally approved course programmes is indirectly or directly prescribed and controlled by professional bodies. By these means the newly qualified professional acquires a complex set of values which:

- define the scope and centrality of the professional in society;
- define the role of the professional in relation to the roles of other professionals in the built environment;
- define what constitutes the legitimate area of concern of the profession.

These value systems are important in explaining the strengths and weaknesses of professional practice, and the extent to which professional practice succeeds in solving the problems of society within the construction and development industry and adapting to new challenges.

WHY IS PROFESSIONAL AUTONOMY DESIRED?

Professional autonomy is a condition desired and maintained by professions. It implies an ability to:

- control entry into the profession;
- define professional standards;
- define the nature of problems and solutions to them;
- act as a pressure group, particularly to influence government;

- command status and rewards;
- define a legitimate field of activity;
- claim exclusive knowledge of the field of activity;
- maintain professional boundaries and define relationships with other professional groups.

This last ability is dependent upon the relative autonomy of other professions in the development and construction industry, and the built environment generally is characterized by interprofessional demarcation disputes. The danger of such disputes is that they reduce the effectiveness of the industry and professional practice, and even the quality of the solution, and ultimately create a poorer built environment.

Chapter 1 describes the objectives of interprofessional collaboration as:

- to break down stereotyped attitudes;
- to improve information flow;
- to improve the decision-making process;
- to avoid abortive work through duplication;
- to increase the cost effectiveness of design procedures.

These objectives may not be realized where interprofessional demarcation disputes are a feature of professional practice.

WHY SHOULD PROFESSIONALS SEEK ALTRUISTIC SERVICE?

One of the characteristic traits of a profession is its commitment to altruistic service, which implies that the beneficiaries of professional activity are other than the professional. Relationships with the client are managed by a code of practice in the private sector and mediated through bureaucratic institutions in the public sector. This raises complex and important issues such as who is the client of professional activity and how the interests and needs of the client are determined.

Without a satisfactory answer to these questions it is difficult to sustain the view that there are altruistic motives underlying professional practice. The concept of altruistic service is a means of legitimizing professional activity in both the public and private sectors for which a professional receives a salary or fee.

WHY IS PROFESSIONAL ACTIVITY PRESENTED AS A TECHNICAL/VALUE NEUTRAL MATTER?

The traditional view of a profession stresses the technical nature of the activity:

- A body of technical knowledge must be acquired.
- Technical objective judgement must be used.

● Decisions are not affected by the values of the decision maker.

This model removes the degree of subjectivity from professional activity and helps to protect the professional from charges of arbitrary and emotional decision making.

This model may be more applicable to certain professional disciplines within the built environment than others. It might be argued that the civil engineer in constructing a bridge relies totally on technical information, whereas a designer interpreting aesthetic taste or a town planner managing land use would apply much more subjective judgements. However, in seeking to conform with the above model, even those professions involved in more subjective judgements may be prone to the use of technical jargon to promote exclusiveness and to protect professional judgement from criticism or examination.

WORKPIECE 2.6

PROFESSIONAL OBJECTIVITY/SUBJECTIVITY

Consider the professional roles listed in Workpiece 2.2 (and any others you are able to identify) and place each role on the continuum of objectivity/subjectivity shown here:

Highly objective _____ Highly subjective
reliance on   reliance on
technical criteria   initiative and judgement

In practice, within an institutional context in the public or private sectors, although the degree of subjectivity of professional activity varies, it is unlikely that any professional activity is devoid of subjective value judgements.

These subjective value judgements may be derived from a variety of sources:

● personal (professional) sources;
● the demands of the client;
● the expressed preferences of the community;
● political judgements in a governmental context.

Here it is useful to make a distinction between public and private sectors. In the private sector, where many of the long-established professions such as the architect or surveyor first appeared, the emphasis lies with a professional code of conduct. The evolving relationships within the private sector will be explored in Chapter 4.

WHO IS THE CLIENT OF PROFESSIONAL ACTIVITY?

In the public sector, where many of the newer professions such as planning and housing management first became established, the situation is much more complex. Here the definition of the public interest takes place within a political context and rarely constitutes a single client. Thus the interests and needs of the client community may be determined in a number of ways, including:

- through political processes involving elected representatives;[4]
- through professionally sponsored public participation.[5]

Public participation has become a central feature of professionalism in the public sector. These complex issues and the pressures placed upon professionals operating in the public sector are explored more fully in Chapter 4.

HOW DO PROFESSIONALS OPERATE IN A BUREAUCRACY?

The majority of professionals, whether in the private or public sectors, work in a bureaucracy. In particular, organizations in the public sector tend to be large complex bureaucracies. The value systems associated with a bureaucratic role may be in conflict with the value systems associated with a professional role. The professional in a bureaucracy may well suffer role conflict.

The bureaucratic role:

- is defined by job description;
- is limited to specialist repetitive activity;
- is set in a hierarchy of roles;
- implies clear lines of reporting;
- implies lack of personal responsibility for outcomes.

(At this point it is recommended that students familiarize themselves with the principles of bureaucratic organization – please refer to the list of further reading at the end of this chapter, especially Haynes.)

In general, professional values acquired through education and training imply a synoptic vision of the activity and individual responsibility for the task. On the other hand, bureaucractic practice regards the professional as instrumental where the task is handled in a corporate manner and team working replaces individual creativity and responsibility.

An example of the sort of role conflicts that may arise is where professional officers are required to present and support in committee policies with which they do not personally agree.

WORKPIECE 2.7

PROFESSIONALISM AND BUREAUCRACY

Define the concepts of professionalism and bureaucracy.
According to these concepts, consider what your response might be to the following questions.

	Values associated with	
	Professionalism	Bureaucracy

1. To what extent do you feel that these values can be acquired through education and training?
2. To what extent do you feel that these values encourage personal responsibility for the task?
3. To what extent do you feel that these values encourage effective team working?
4. To what extent do you feel that these values encourage or inhibit effective collaboration between professionals?
5. What are the main areas of conflict?

THE DEVELOPMENT OF PROFESSIONAL FASHIONS

Professions are very important in developing policy solutions to complex problems. They seek the autonomy to be able to define current best practice. Many of the solutions adopted do not derive from the client but are produced within professional circles with the application of purely professional values.

Professionals sharing similar values and views of current best practice work in many public and private organizations, central and local government and private practice. Some authors have pointed to the interpenetration of values between the public and private sectors of a profession[6] and others have developed the idea of policy communities to explain the development of periodic professional fashions.[7]

PROFESSIONAL BOUNDARIES AND MULTIDISCIPLINARY PRACTICE

The process of professionalization may imply an attempt to define ever wider professional boundaries. This process is likely to cause demarcation disputes between professions. Some classic examples are: disputes between architects and planners over responsibility for urban design, between environmental health officers and housing professionals over urban renewal, between engineers and planners over highway issues, and between architects, building surveyors and building engineers in building construction.

Professions may seek to enclose the disputed territory within their professional boundaries artificially, thus causing interprofessional conflict and demarcation disputes. Alternatively the disputed territory can be handled in a different way by interprofessional collaboration and a multidisciplinary approach to the task. In the public sector of local government the application of corporate management approaches[8] was designed to break down professional barriers and establish multidisciplinary approaches to policy making. In the private sector the establishment of a multidisciplinary team is described in Chapter 1 as part of innovative collaborative practice.

If applied rigidly, the development of professional approaches may have more disadvantages than advantages. The limitations and problems associated with professionalism explored in this chapter imply that a more open and positive approach to interprofessional collaboration would be advantageous. An understanding of the strengths and weaknesses of the concept of professionalism supports the development of value systems encouraging and supporting interprofessional collaboration. The search for new and innovative professional roles and relationships will be unnecessarily constrained by rigid adherence to traditional notions of a profession and professional roles.

SUMMARY

The purpose of this chapter has been to explore some of the basic features behind the concept of a profession and to demonstrate the strengths and weaknesses of a traditional view of a specialist professional.

WORKPIECE 2.8

INTERPROFESSIONAL RELATIONSHIPS

Take a profession that you are particularly interested in and examine its relationship with other professional groups. Refer to the diagram in the worked example for the planning profession in local government.

Instructions:

1. Place subject profession in circle.
2. Identify other professions around perimeter.
3. Identify disputed territory in segments.

Consider whether the disputed territory in the segments should be colonized or artificially enclosed in one profession or whether these areas of activity can be handled in a more collaborative fashion.

Worked example of interprofessional relationships for planning profession in local government.

The processes whereby value systems are established and reinforced have been described. The value systems associated with particular professional groups largely determine the extent to which a particular profession is able to engage in the sort of emerging collaborative practices described in this book. Finally this chapter, in view of the limitations of the definition of a traditional specialist profession, advocates a more flexible interprofessional approach to professional activity in the future.

CHECKLIST

- What is a profession?
- When is an occupation regarded as a profession?
- Does a professional have a well defined area of interest?
- What is the role of education and training?
- Why is professional autonomy desired?
- Why should professionals seek altruistic service?
- Why is professional activity presented as a technical/value neutral matter?
- Who is the client of professional activity?
- How do professionals operate in a bureaucracy?
- The development of professional fashions.
- Professional boundaries and multidisciplinary practice.

REFERENCES

1. Millerson, G. (1964) *The Qualifying Association*, Routledge and Kegan Paul.
2. Johnson, T.J. (1972) *Professions and Power*, Macmillan.
3. Laffin, M. (1986) *Professionalism and Policy: The role of the professions in the central/local government relationship*, Gower.
4. Gyford, J., Leach, S. and Game, C. (1989) *The Changing Politics of Local Government*, Unwin Hyman, London.
5. Boaden, N., Goldsmith, M., Hampton, W. and Stringer, P. (1982) *Public Participation in Local Services*, Longman, London.
6. Dunleavy, P. (1980) *Urban Political Analysis*, Macmillan.
7. Rhodes, R.A.W. (1986) *The National World of Local Government*, Allen & Unwin.
8. Stewart, J.D. (1972) *Management in Local Government: A viewpoint*, Charles Knight.

FURTHER READING

Dunleavy, P. (1981) *The politics of mass housing in Britain 1945–75: Corporate power and professional influence in the Welfare State*, Clarendon Press.

Haynes, R.J. (1980) *Organization theory and local government*, Allen & Unwin.

Laffin, M. and Young, K. (1990) *Professionalism in Local Government*, Longman.

CHAPTER THREE

INTERPROFESSIONAL COLLABORATION IN THE PRIVATE SECTOR

TOM MUIR

THEME

This chapter explores the development of the private professional office from the industrialized society of the nineteenth century. It discusses that office's position in relation to the changing scale of development ushered in by the twentieth century and how the private sector adapted to changing practices and changing society. The theme counterpoints the more traditional private sector professional with the public sector interprofessional officer and discusses how each responded to demands for an interprofessional service.

OBJECTIVES

After reading this chapter you should be able to:

● understand the nature of traditional private practice for a built environment professional such as an architect, engineer, quantity surveyor, estate manager, landscape architect;

● trace how private practice has adapted to the new conditions in the twentieth century;

● be aware of how the private sector responded to the need for cooperative professional services for large projects;

● be aware of the commercial nature of operating a professional office in the private sector;

- understand the wide difference that exists in character between small and large private practices.

The traditional role of the private sector in the development process has undergone massive changes due to the changing context in which it operates. In particular the growth of the public sector in the twentieth century has had a considerable impact on the private sector. As a consequence, different types of private professional practices have had to adapt to these new circumstances. The culmination of these changes is demonstrated by the emergence of the large interprofessional practice which is well suited to the complexities of the development process within the construction and development industry.

Prior to the twentieth century there was little concept of any sector other than the private sector. It was the development of local government armed with the right to tax, and charged with implementing major legislation such as the great public health and housing acts of the latter part of the nineteenth century that laid the basis for a major public sector involvement by the built environment profession.

When the public sector did develop, however, it grew quickly and at its height employed possibly as many as 25–30% of all built environment professionals. This meant that those operating in the private sector found themselves working under quite a different concept of professionalism. Although commercial and business interests remained of prime importance, the private sector was now confronted with a large number of their fellow professionals salaried and working for local or central government.

In the early part of this century the normal activities of the various professions in the construction and development industry were carried out in relatively small offices. These professionals acted as consultants to the appropriate sector of the industry and established themselves as an integral part of the social and economic fabric of their community.

After the 1914–18 war, government (both local and central) began to have an increasing involvement in urban development. Local authorities in particular established larger departments to handle the increasing work load brought about through legislation in education, town and country planning, building control and housing management. New devolved responsibilities in education and housing generated a demand for professionally trained specialists in all areas.

These important social and political events coincided with major changes in the socio-economic structure of society which in turn coincided with dramatic changes within the construction and development industry itself. Rapid developments in technology 'borrowed' from other industries (such as munitions) put severe pressure on the traditional small professional office. Many of them found themselves ill equipped to cope with either the scale of the new projects or the level of complexity that they demanded.

Some local authorities set up large multiprofessional technical services departments which enabled architects, planners, engineers, quantity surveyors and building surveyors to operate in flexible ways; others retained a degree of independence. However, the umbrella of a single employer allowed a wider range of optional cooperation. These developments in the public sector were reflected by similar developments in the private sector.

WORKPIECE 3.1

THE ADVANTAGES AND DISADVANTAGES OF LOCATION IN THE PRIVATE SECTOR

Select a small private professional practice of the profession with which you are most familiar and list precisely what you think are the advantages and disadvantages of it being in the private sector.

Now prepare two similar lists indicating your perception of the advantages and disadvantages of the same professional operating in a public office.

THE NATURE OF PRIVATE PROFESSIONAL PRACTICES

We might identify the following as a typical range of practice configurations found in the private sector:[1]

● The small-scale practice
● The medium-size office
● The large interprofessional practice.

THE SMALL-SCALE PRACTICE

The small-scale practice normally consists of one or two principals and possibly an assistant plus clerical support. This office represents more clearly the inherited tradition of the 'community' professional (rather like the general practitioner in medicine). The practice now predominantly handles small jobs and tends to be more commonly found in rural or semi-rural areas. This type of practice can often prove remarkably resilient when faced with diminishing work loads due to low overheads and clear, if limited, targeted project scale.

THE MEDIUM-SIZE OFFICE

The medium-size office offers a single professional service with perhaps four or five partners, and possibly eight to ten assistants plus clerical support. Such an office should, in theory, be capable of dealing with the largest of projects but, with the changes in client demand and the increasingly high specialist content in projects, this size of office has proved to be the most vulnerable. Many either split up and moved to smaller projects or changed the composition of their staffing profile so as to offer a multiprofessional service.

THE LARGE INTERPROFESSIONAL PRACTICE

Large interprofessional groups are set up on the model of a local authority technical services department but offer a whole range of professional services including planning consultancy, design, project management, cost advice, facilities management and many more.

These have proved extremely adaptable and responsive to the changes in requirements of different types of projects. Some proved flexible enough to be planning consultants to new towns while taking on relatively small architectural commissions and giving engineering consultancy to other projects.

Their weaknesses tend to be the size and relatively high minimum economic base required to sustain them. Many over the last few years have dramatically scaled down their size due to the lack of suitable large projects.

WORKPIECE 3.2

PRIVATE PROFESSIONAL COMPARISONS

We have discussed the advantages and disadvantages of a small one or two person professional practice. Select two such small practices representing different built environment professions.

Analyse each in terms of the following criteria:

- Overall workload capacity.
- Financial stability over 1 year and 5 years.
- Range of projects which can be undertaken effectively.
- Work patterns with other built environment professions.

Compare them with each other, noting where the different aspects of their respective professional practices create different conditions.

Draw some conclusions from your studies as to how small professional practices fit into the current climate in the built environment – particularly in terms of interprofessional collaborations.

HOW HAVE PRIVATE PROFESSIONAL PRACTICES ADAPTED TO CURRENT CIRCUMSTANCES?

The three examples given above have, by necessity, simplified a wide range of different practice sizes but they do represent a clear distinction in market position. Let us examine how each has responded to the situations and conditions which they are currently encountering.

THE SMALL-SCALE PRACTICE

As mentioned before, these practices can be remarkably resilient to changing economic climates but they have an inbuilt inflexibility in the nature of the service they can provide. Small practices tend to be less viable as they cannot justify the employment of specialist skills. Although they can survive downturns in workload, they do have to absorb the losses personally and can often find themselves significantly underemployed and therefore underpaid. Several different options are open to small practices to increase their viability and yet still maintain their individual character. They might:

- become an independent 'branch' of a large national group;
- create a consortium of local practices;
- form a multidisciplinary consortium;[2]
- link with contractor.

INDEPENDENT BRANCH OF A LARGE NATIONAL GROUP   This would allow the practice both to exploit the staff skills across the group and possibly gain work in other parts of the country while still retaining a local identity. There is some loss in independence, however, as it is likely that some common financial 'base' would be required. Also policy decisions are unlikely to be the prerogative of the local situation.

CONSORTIUM OF LOCAL PRACTICES   This creates a more variable labour 'pool' and would allow much greater flexibility in both the range and number of projects which can be undertaken.

MULTIDISCIPLINARY CONSORTIUM   This would allow them to offer a fully integrated service to a client and might include architectural, quantity surveying, structural engineering, landscape or other services. Such a move would be a positive response to an increasingly acknowledged fact that clients would prefer to deal with one group representing all professional services rather than four, five or even more individual professionals, which was the traditional model.

LINKING WITH CONTRACTOR   Carrying the previous option one stage further, an office might link not just with the other professionals but with the contractor. This would apparently provide the client with the optimum situation whereby contact has to be maintained with only one organization. One of the criticisms of such an arrangement is the absorption of what has traditionally been the objective roles played by the professionals into the contract stage. As a result the client may be more vulnerable in cases of dispute between client and contractor.

In summary, the small professional office can be viable even in an era of large-scale projects and programmes. However, in order to be so, partners or principals must be realistic with the objectives, recognize the limitations of the practice and be prepared to consider innovative options if the situation should arise.

Over recent years this size of office has proved most vulnerable to the decline in building or planning projects. Medium-size offices have found that, due to the unpredictability of staffing, their office 'profile' can be either top heavy with too many partners or unbalanced between professional and technical support staff. This balance is critical as it governs not only the type and range of projects which can be undertaken but also the financial viability of their operation. Some options available to such practices in response to the shifting character of the present development industry are to:

● broaden the professional skills of the office;
● incorporate project management skills;
● become a developer and generate its own projects;
● link with a developer;
● form a single-project consortium.

BROADENING PROFESSIONAL SKILLS   By doing this, a much wider range of projects can be undertaken and a more comprehensive and coordinated professional service can be provided. An added advantage is that each additional profession represented in the practice can provide a service of work through its own particular skills. This allows the practice to offer:

● an integrated multiprofessional service;
● specific professional consultancy skills to other projects.

THE MEDIUM-SIZE OFFICE

INCORPORATING PROJECT MANAGEMENT SKILLS

The incorporation of project management skills can help to create new work in its own right and provide opportunities for further consultancy services to be offered to other offices.

BECOMING A DEVELOPER By incorporating estate management skills into, say, an architectural/surveying practice, projects can be procured, financed, built, managed and sold, thus providing both employment and continuing income to the practice. It also develops a strong sense of 'total' responsibility when the office is its own client.

LINKING WITH A DEVELOPER As with the small-scale practice, a consortium with a developer can be formed in which the particular professional skills of the practice are incorporated into a 'package deal' or design/build programme. This has the same strengths and weaknesses outlined above for small practices.

SINGLE-PROJECT CONSORTIUM As with the small-scale practice, a single-project consortium can be formed. However, a multiprofessional practice of medium size might only have to link with one or two to be able to provide a full range of professional services for any contract.

This size and type of practice demands a high work turnover to remain solvent, particularly in the case of practices with a multiprofessional partnership and staff. Each profession requires a different turnover rate to maintain full employment, therefore such practices are governed by those staff which require the highest cost-effective workload. In the development boom of the 1960s and 1970s, such practices had no problems sustaining and in fact increasing their workforce. In the latter part of the 1980s and in the 1990s the cut-back in building dramatically affected them and many tended to break up and reform into smaller, often single professional groupings. Many simply set up single-person practices operating out of their homes, thereby minimizing overheads.

LARGE INTERPROFESSIONAL PRACTICE

In the immediate post-war period major development programmes designed to renew the physical fabric of our cities were undertaken. These took the form of:

● massive new house building programmes utilizing the latest methods of building systems and being designed and laid out under totally new principles;

THE ROLE OF PRINCIPAL OR PARTNER IN A PRIVATE PROFESSIONAL PRACTICE

The working life of principals or partners in private professional practices frequently covers a very wide range of activities of which only a few seem to relate directly to the nature of their prime professional skill.

Interview a principal or partner in a private professional practice and make a detailed analysis of a typical week. Your analysis should identify the amount of time spent:

● carrying out prime professional activities (and define those activities);

● doing administration;
● managing;
● travelling;
● on public relations;
● in office and out of office;
● doing professional activities other than the one trained in.

Indicate what conclusions you personally draw from the results of your analysis.

● new 'green field' universities involving complex demands and requiring not only new building methods but completely new 'business orientated' approaches to project management;
● new hospital building programmes in which the engineering and technical content of the building demanded an integrated approach by the design team.

In addition to these major programmes, the 1946 New Town Act initiated a series of New Town projects of a scale and character never previously encountered within the development and construction industry. The vehicle created to implement this policy was the Development Corporation, which was independent from local authorities and acted as an agent for central government.

Development corporations set up organizations employing a small range of 'urban' specialists with chief officers from social and economic development, housing, education, industrial development, health services and architecture and planning. The former worked as a client body for the architects and planners but, because they all worked for the same corporation, a corporate team developed.

The development corporation was designated for a fixed period of time after which, when its job was completed, the 'new town' was handed over to the appropriate local authority and the corporation was disbanded. Often the staff from the architecture and development office established private practices based upon their previous experiences and continued with their interdisciplinary working practices.

The initial plan for the new town was normally commissioned by the development corporation from a private consultant. Commissions of this size and scale were a major stimulant to the development industry. By their very nature these commissions demanded interdisciplinary teams for their execution. Two of the basic demands of central government for new town plans were that they should be 'effective' and 'practical'. In many cases large, multidisciplinary practices were established in response to these commissions and professional staff including planners, architects, developers, quantity surveyors, landscape architects, transportation engineers, social scientists, economists and others found employment in them.

INTERNATIONAL OPERATORS   Such practices encountered the problem of variable professional workload requirements as mentioned above for the medium-size office and the response usually was to become an international operator. Firms such as Robert Matthew, Johnson–Marshall and Partners (now RMJM Ltd), Ove Arup (Arup Associates), Colin Buchanan and Partners, Llewellyn Davis, Forrestier and Partners, Weeks and Bor and others all took this path and ultimately finished up in the late 1970s as major multinational, multiprofessional consultancies in the private sector. Although they are all truly multiprofessional, they developed from different professional bases.

Their office structures varied too although most of them retained a single monolithic practice character with offices spread throughout the world. This resulted in teams being established for specific projects with professional skills appropriate to the demands of the job. In nearly every case, there was a 'main' office and all others were 'branches'.

One interesting variation on this pattern was Building Design Partnership (BDP) which at one stage in the late 1970s to early 1980s was the largest multidisciplinary practice in the country. This practice evolved a system of establishing offices throughout the UK and abroad, which were 'franchised' to the corporate practice of BDP. This allowed local offices to develop in response to local conditions, but when appropriate exploit the full interprofessional capacity of the corporate practice. It also allowed for highly flexible cash management between small local practices and the large corporate international identity of BDP.

The interesting contrast between the former models and BDP can be traced back to their origins. All practices previously mentioned were founded by former local authority officers and, not surprisingly, set up in a manner somewhat similar to a local authority department. BDP's founder, however, was always in the private sector and his 'franchise' system is a marriage between traditional small practice methods and the larger multiprofessional consultancy, philosophies to which the founder was totally committed.

An office which offers another route to multiprofessional practice is Ove Arup and Partners. They originated in engineering practice but gradually moved towards incorporating design consultancy and eventually established an 'offshoot' practice called Arup Associates which evolved as a major multidisciplinary design group in its own right. The characteristic form of interdisciplinary work in Arup Associates was small, interprofessional project teams, their leaders being generated from within the team, which exploited the resources and reputation of the parent practice of Ove Arup. This approach has already been discussed in Chapter 1.

THE GROWTH OF MORE PRAGMATIC PRACTICES

These large design and planning practices reflected the growth and perhaps idealism of the post-war period. Since the mid 1980s the equivalent growth in professional consultancies in the built environment has been in the more pragmatic areas of cost control, management consultancy and project management. Several large national consultancies have developed strong reputations in such areas. Bucknall Austin, Francis Graves and Partners, E.C. Harris and Davies, Langdon and Everest are four such practices. Each of these grew not from the design/planning disciplines but from quantity surveying.

The essential requirement of professionalism in the private sector is the basic need for financial solvency. This has always been the case and remains so today. However, the nature of public accountability currently holding sway in local government, and other public authorities, has resulted in even public sector professionals having to act in commercially 'competitive' ways. Chapter 4 considers this more recent privatization phase in more detail. It could be argued that the commercial imperative is not always the best criterion for good practice in development processes, but it is an essential component. Within the private sector much debate centres on the degree of independence required of each discipline within a project. There would appear to be conflicting advantages and disadvantages in either situation.

This service offers the client the maximum in independent professional advice as normally each consultant is directly responsible only to the

HOW INDEPENDENT CAN PRIVATE SECTOR PROFESSIONALS BE?

FULLY INDEPENDENT PROFESSIONALS

client while still working with the other members of the team.[3] Often such appointments are made upon the advice of one or other of the consultants, but when the team is established each member is responsible to the client. The main advantage in this is the objectivity of the advice the client would receive from consultants whereby each consultant advises the client directly as to what their best interests are in the area of the consultant's expertise.

A possible disadvantage is that a substantial amount of knowledge, competence and time could be required of the client in coordinating this information and optimizing potentially conflicting advice from different consultants.

Another likely disadvantage is that this type of arrangment does not actively encourage effective team working and may on occasions discourage it, resulting in additional cost. In most projects, professional consultants who have worked before on previous projects are assembled, thus building on established working relationships. It is not, however, an effective arrangement to serve the demand of the present development industry in which the ability to complete a project on time, at the right price and of the agreed quality is paramount.

PROJECT-LINKED CONSULTANCIES

In these arrangements, as explained previously, each practice retains its own integrity as an office but links up with other types of consultant to offer an integrated service for a particular project. This can offer the best of both worlds as it enables a practice to carry out larger and more complex jobs working in interprofessional teams while retaining the independence of its own professional base.

THE EVOLUTION OF PRIVATE SECTOR INTERPROFESSIONAL PRACTICE

The evolution of private sector interprofessional practice professions can be identified in the following sequence:

- Very little prior to the twentieth century as most professionals worked from relatively small single-professional offices. These offices employed people with additional skills but little can be deduced as several of the professional bodies did not exist then.
- With the arrival of the twentieth century came housing and town planning roles for local government, along with building controls and housing management. New local authorities became the first real examples of interdisciplinary collaboration.
- New professions such as quantity surveyors, housing managers, town planners and building surveyors became institutionalized,

thereby putting interprofessional collaboration on a more formal basis. Often a client would have three or more different professionals as consultants on one project.

- Increasingly sophisticated technology in buildings and in cities served to narrow even further the specialized skills of each profession. An example of how a profession has responded to such changes is the Royal Institution of Chartered Surveyors. From a single monolithic body established in the 1860s, it was broken down into the following divisions:

    Land – land hydrographics, minerals, rural
    Property – general practice, planning and development
    Construction – quantity surveyors, building surveyors.

- The same increasing sophistication of technology eventually began to demand more collaboration between professional teams in development projects. In some buildings, for example, the building services element, traditionally the work of the mechanical and electrical engineers, could comprise up to 80% of the total cost. Such development has led to the growth of a new division of engineers called 'building services' which is aimed at designing the total services engineering needs of a building within one discipline.

In general, what we see in this chapter is that two often conflicting forces are exerting pressure on the individual professional practice:

- The need to acquire ever more complex and specific technical knowledge about an industry which, through increasingly sophisticated materials and transferred technologies, is becoming beyond any one person's capacity to 'keep up'.
- The wish of both the industry and clients for a single-focus management structure within which an interdisciplinary team operates across professional barriers.

This is the challenge for the private practice of the future. Failure to respond will almost inevitably reduce the practice to being that of the technician rather than professional. However, this kind of demarcation is likely to change as the roles of professionals and technicians develop and new collaborative practices emerge. We have already discussed this in Chapter 2. We now need to look at the changing roles of the public sector in Chapter 4.

SUMMARY

This chapter has discussed the development of professional practice in the private sector in response to the changing demands and challenges placed on private sector professionals. It describes how modern collaborative practice is necessary to respond to current challenges facing the construction and development industry and traces how the nature and focus of practices have varied. It illustrates how the professions themselves have changed and ways in which these changes have impacted in private practice.

CHECKLIST

The issues covered in this chapter are:

- how the growth of the public sector has affected private practice;
- the nature of private professional practices;
- how private professional practices have adapted to current circumstances;
- how independent the private sector professionals can be;
- the evolution of private sector interprofessional practice.

REFERENCES

1. Thompson, F.M.C. (1968) *Chartered Surveyors: The Growth of a Profession*, Routledge.
2. Minale, M. (1991) *How to run a successful multidisciplinary design company*, Eflandart.
3. Kaderlan, N. (1991) *Designing your Practice*, McGraw-Hill.

FURTHER READING

ACA (1988) *Project Team Guidelines: Fee Negotiations and Harmonised Plans of Work*, ACA, London.

Bates, J. and Hally, D. (1982) *The Financing of Small Business*, Sweet and Maxwell.

Chappell, D. and Willis, C. (1992) *The Architect in Practice*, 7th edn, Blackwell Scientific.

Chiddick, D. and Millington, A. (1984) *Land Management: New Directions*, E & FN Spon.

Gutway, R. (1992) *Architectural Practice*, Princeton Architectural Press.

Katz, B. (1992) *Selling Professional Services*, Gower.

Moxley, R. (1993) *Building Management by Professionals*, Butterworth.

Centre for Strategic Studies (1988) *Building Britain 2001*, University of Reading.

The Surveyors 500, 2nd edn, Tuckers Directories, Manchester.

Watson, J. (1973) The Incompleat Surveyor, *Estates Gazette*.

Watson, J. (1977) *The Savills: A family and a firm*, Hutchinson.

THE CHANGING ROLE OF THE PUBLIC SECTOR AND THE EFFECT OF EUROPEAN LEGISLATION ON LOCAL GOVERNMENT

CHAPTER FOUR

BRIAN RANCE, WITH A CONTRIBUTION FROM DR DAVID SHAW

THEME

This chapter is concerned with the major contextual features which are forcing a re-evaluation of the role of the professional officer in the public sector. Changes in the roles of professional officers in local government, which are considered in some detail, are mirrored by changes in the roles of professional civil servants and other public sector professionals. The role of the public sector in the development process is adapting to meet these significant trends. Local authorities in particular have a critical enabling role, but rarely nowadays initiate large development projects themselves in isolation from other partners in the public and private sector. Connections can be made with Part One of Book 2 in this series (*Design, Technology and the Development Process in the Built Environment*) which explores relationships between the use of design and the appreciation of technology in a social, political and economic context.

OBJECTIVES

After reading this chapter you should be able to:

● understand the changing institutional context in which built environment professionals operate within the public sector;

● appreciate the ways in which public sector professional bureaucrats are adapting their role;

● understand the contribution of these developments to breaking down stereotyped professional roles and the emergence of collaborative practice.

INTRODUCTION

The traditional role of the public sector as an initiator of development has largely ceased. Local authorities do not by and large hold significant land banks or undertake substantial development projects. Central government policy, through legislation, circular advice and financial controls, has encouraged local authorities to see themselves as enablers of development rather than direct providers. This enabling role implies the provision of a development service within a framework of legal controls. For example, a potential development must still secure planning permission but the renovation of a council housing estate may well be put out to tender within the framework of legislation relating to compulsory competitive tendering.

In addition to the changing role of local authorities, the distribution of functions within the public sector and between the public and private sector has changed significantly. One of the central planks of government policy over the last decade has been the privatization of public services, where responsibility for provision has been transferred to the private sector. Also government policy has resulted in many new single-service quangos (quasi autonomous non-governmental organizations) being set up in more complex interagency relationships within the public sector. For example, the abolition of the metropolitan counties in 1986 resulted in the creation of joint boards outside the control of local authorities.

Within the context of these institutional changes, the traditional role of the local authority built environment professional has had to be adapted. New relationships have been forged with professionals working in the private sector and in dealing with professionals in other public sector agencies. In addition, public sector professional bureaucrats now have to operate within an increasingly European context and have to face the challenges associated with an increasingly politicized climate in local government. As a result the concept of professionalism and the role of the public sector professional bureaucrat are being re-examined.

Privatization has been defined as 'a set of policies which aim to limit the role of the public sector, and increase the role of the private sector, while improving the performance of the remaining public sector'.[1] This definition identifies the requirement for local authorities to adopt a more market-oriented approach to their role as well as encouraging the 'hiving off' of functions to the private sector.

Stoker[2] identifies three forms of privatization:

- Selling off local authority assets.
- Deregulation and competitive tendering.
- Encouraging private sector provision and investment.

Selling off local authority assets includes such policies as the sale of land owned by the local authority and the selling of council houses under the 'right to buy' policy. The deregulation policy mainly applies to bus services. Perhaps the potentially most far-reaching of measures are contained within compulsory competitive tendering and these are dealt with in more detail below. The more nebulous encouragement of private sector provision and investment are common in the fields of housing, urban renewal and economic regeneration and include such initiatives as urban development corporations, enterprise zones and housing action trusts; they normally take the form of partnerships between public and private sectors.

Although the 1988 Local Government Act is an important milestone, there is no one piece of legislation or policy statement that summarizes the government's approach. However, this approach has been described as one of 'rolling back the frontiers of the State' and has been ascribed to the very influential 'new right philosophy'.[3]

In essence the policy is an economic one linked with 'monetarism' which is concerned to reduce public expenditure, reduce the inflationary effect of taxation and make the management of the economy more

THE PRIVATIZATION OF LOCAL AUTHORITY ROLES

effective. The singular achievement of the 'new right philosophy' is in identifying local government as the main culprit in this 'overspending'.[3] Thus privatization policies as applied to local government are designed to reduce public expenditure and the need for taxation to support public expenditure. As a consequence the burden of taxation will be lifted from the private sector, thus making it more efficient and profitable, and better able to provide services formerly provided by the public sector.

This philosophy, in one form or another, has shaped the emerging structure and organization of the public sector in recent years. It is one of the contextual developments that has caused public sector professional bureaucrats to re-evaluate their role in service provision in the field of the built environment.

THE EFFECT OF COMPULSORY COMPETITIVE TENDERING

Over the last decade, perhaps the single most influential and far-reaching privatization measure affecting the role of the professional officer in local government has been the progressive introduction of compulsory competitive tendering. Although the 'contracting out' of local government services is not a new phenomenon, the compulsory requirement is a substantial new development.[4]

Provision for compulsory competitive tendering was originally introduced in the 1980 Local Government Land and Planning Act but was restricted to certain services such as waste disposal and certain functions like cleaning and catering. The idea was that local authority manual workers were required to organize themselves into direct labour organizations to compete for local authority contracts. Local authorities would be able to achieve an economic service and maintain the quality of the service (that is, securing 'value for money') by administering the contracting process. In this way local authorities have increasingly become managers of contractual relations rather than direct service providers. The success of the private sector in bidding for local authority contracts has become an even more important element in sustaining the local economy.[5]

The 1988 Local Government Act contained provisions to enable the Secretary of State to widen the list of services subject to compulsory competitive tendering procedures. In recent years this privatization initiative has gained considerable momentum, with most local authorities significantly affected. So far the major impact has been on the manual workforce and has not directly affected the professional officer in terms of employment prospects. Nevertheless the service task may have changed and many professionals are increasingly involved in managing the contract rather than in planning direct provision.

Consideration has been given to the extension of compulsory competitive tendering procedures to professional services. Potentially this could have far-reaching effects for professionals directly concerned with managing the development process in local government. For some years local authorities, because they rarely undertake development themselves, have not required large teams of architects or construction professionals. Now it is conceivable that services like building control, development control and development planning could be 'contracted out' in the future. Already there have been examples of local plan preparation being contracted out to planning consultants.[6] If the current trend towards privatization of local authority services continues unabated the balance of professionals employed in public and private sectors could change radically. For example, the consultancy sector in planning which is currently relatively small, but growing, could increase massively in the short and medium term.

The more market-oriented approach to the public sector has led central government to question the idea of an all-purpose local authority in the sense of a local democratic institution with the fullest range of devolved functions. Instead government policy has tendered to favour the creation of a range of single function or area specific non-democratic bodies to administer local services. There has been a substantial growth in these intergovernmental agencies in the name of breaking the public sector monopoly of local government. This increase in quangos has come about from two sources:

- Functions transferred from local authorities.
- Functions created by government in response to new legislation.

As a consequence of these changes, any development project is more likely to involve a range of public sector agencies with different purposes. The effective coordination of multiple public sector agencies becomes a critical consideration in any development project.

THE EMERGENCE OF INTERAGENCY GOVERNMENT

THE POLITICIZATION OF LOCAL GOVERNMENT

Many commentators have reported and tried to define a fundamental trend in local government today which is referred to as politicization. By one means or another the relationship between elected members and professional officers is undergoing a fundamental change. In essence this is reflected in a changing 'power balance' between members and officers, where the increasing influence of members in decision making has meant that traditional professional roles have been subjected to a

WORKPIECE 4.I

INTERAGENCY RELATIONSHIPS

Discuss any development project you may be familiar with and analyse the involvement of various agencies of government, the private sector and the community in the development process by using the given pro forma.

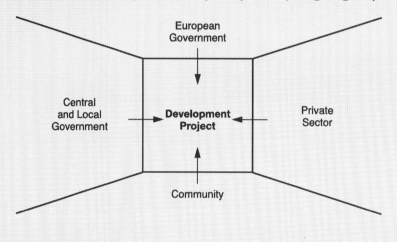

re-examination. In many large urban local authorities, where the trend to politicization is most marked, officers are having to redefine their professional roles.

Because of the inner contradictions of the concept of professionalism referred to in Chapter 2, it is difficult for officers to resist pressure to adapt their role and defend traditional concepts of professionalism. The concept of professionalism, which has been nurtured over the years and has served local government well under extreme pressure, is undergoing a process of redefinition.[7]

The practical effect of these changes is that the traditional autonomy of the professional officer to determine and implement policy decisions is being eroded. The traditional view of member/officer relations has been described as the 'dictatorship of the official'[8] where the professional officer was able to determine policy and control decision making and elected members were largely passive, using committee processes in effect to 'rubber stamp' officer decisions. More often nowadays with the increasing politicization of local government,[9] the elected member is much more active in decision making. It is not unusual for members to overturn officer recommendations in committee, control the content of committee agendas, and to vet reports and proposals put forward by professional officers before they reach the committee stage.

The trend to increasing politicization has constrained the traditional autonomy given to the professional officers to determine and implement policy decisions in local government. As a consequence professional officers have had to adapt their role to this more highly charged political atmosphere and seek to collaborate in new relationships with elected members. These new relationships are only possible if professional officers are willing and able to redefine their professional role away from the traditional model described in Chapter 2.

New forms of partnership have emerged between members and officers and the establishment of member/officer working groups has become more common. Normally these working groups are set up to manage a particular project with members and officers working together. Sometimes other partners, members of the community and representatives of other agencies and interests may be coopted as part of the team. Political support becomes a key element in the success of any development project.

In 1972 the UK became part of the European Economic Community (EEC) and over time this supranational organization has had an ever increasing impact on the way local government operates. Enshrined within the Treaty of Rome of 1957 were the four freedoms: that people, goods, services and capital should have free mobility throughout the member states. In the first 20 years of European integration, progress towards these freedoms was slow. In 1985 the heads of government committed themselves to achieving a single market progressively between 1985 and the end of 1992. This was formerly enshrined in the Single European Act of 1987. More recently, the process of European integration has been reinforced with the signing of the Treaty of Union (more commonly known as Maastricht) in 1992 and its ratification by the 12 member states. In 1995 the 12 were extended to 15 and in 1996 there will be further discussion between the heads of government with the aim of progressing towards a principle of the original treaty, namely that there should be a closer relationship between member states.

In signing and ratifying the major bilateral treaties of Rome, the Single European Act and Maastricht, each member state agrees to cede some sovereign powers, in so far as they agree to abide by and implement European-wide legislation for as long as they are part of the European Union. The changing nature and power of European integration is in

THE EFFECT OF EUROPEAN LEGISLATION ON LOCAL GOVERNMENT

part reflected in the names given to the 'supra-European state'.[10]

In 1972 the UK joined the European Economic Community; by the mid 1980s the economic element had been dropped and the organization was described as the European Community; since 1993 we have all been citizens of the European Union. Now that we are subject to European law, the Union has had, and is likely to have, a significant impact on the way that local government professionals operate. The impact can be divided into three main areas of concern:

- Direct impact
- Funding
- Distribution of economic benefits.

DIRECT IMPACT   There is a direct impact on the way that organizations operate in terms of processes and procedures. For example: public procurement regulations require local professionals to advertise projects of more than £150 000 on a European-wide basis; or in the field of environmental management there are obligations on service/utilities providers (e.g. water) to meet certain minimum standards with respect to protecting and improving the environment; or for major development proposals the project needs to be subjected to an environmental impact assessment.

FUNDING   Secondly, there is the impact of the Community Structural Funds, namely the European Regional Development Fund, the Social Fund and the Guidance section of the Regional Development Fund. In the case of the European Social Fund, money is available for all regions to assist training and retraining schemes for disadvantaged groups including the long-term unemployed, women returning to work, disabled individuals, etc. The other two programmes are specifically targeted at areas of considerable disadvantage. For example, Merseyside is an objective 1 area where the Gross Domestic Product is less than 75% of the Community average; the West Midlands is an objective 2 area suffering traditional industrial decline and needing help and support in economic restructuring; and remote rural areas such as Mid-Wales and the Highlands of Scotland have objective 5 status where the emphasis is to provide alternative enterprises for agriculture and improve basic services. Between 1989 and 1993 this amounted to 793 million Ecu of European assistance for funding various projects, much of which was channelled through the local authorities.

DISTRIBUTION OF ECONOMIC BENEFITS   The process of European integration, the promotion of transnational European transport networks and the movement towards a single unified market are all expected to produce major macro-economic benefits. These are unlikely to be evenly distributed and thus new developments are likely to be more concentrated in some areas to the relative disadvantage of others. Rapid new growth in the economies of the northern Mediterranean region from Milan through to Barcelona is already being experienced. This will increasingly require local authorities to think strategically in a local/regional/national and increasingly European/international context in order to maintain their relative position.

In acknowledging that European legislation is having a greater impact on the way that local government professionals operate, there are several issues that the organization needs to address at the corporate level.

ISSUES FOR LOCAL AUTHORITIES

AWARENESS   Are all officers and members aware of the role, functions and competencies of the European Union? Does the concept of subsidiarity (which means that decisions should be made at the most appropriate local level) imply a strengthening of the role of regional and local authorities in decision making?

IMPACT   Are all officers aware of the competencies of the European Union to produce legislation which may have an impact on the way in which they operate? These can be seen as direct impacts on all activities. In addition to the promotion of its policies and programmes, many initiatives are supported by various funding programmes to create employment opportunities, invest in infrastructure and promote exchanges and understanding of different European cultures. Also as a result of European integration as well as the broader globalization of economic activity, the local authority needs to be much more aware of the external factors shaping its potential success.

IMPORTANCE   There is so much information and material and there are so many policies and proposals emanating from the European Union that it is important to determine what is important. This requires resources to be devoted to keeping a watching brief in terms of what is going on. Many local authorities now have a European Unit to monitor policy and opportunities for funding projects and some large authorities (e.g Birmingham and Strathclyde) or groups of authorities (e.g the East

Midlands) have employed staff permanently in Brussels to safeguard their interests. The Audit Commission estimates that the cost of employing a lobbyist is in excess of £100 000 per annum.

Clearly, European integration is having a greater impact on the organization and operation of local government than is generally acknowledged. Indeed it is argued that some of the major legislation in the UK is shaped by European thinking behind the Environmental Protection Act. Furthermore, the UK policy of compulsory competitive tendering is still subject to European law, as a recent case relating to job security and wage levels for contracted out staff serves to testify.

The rapid change and the increasing impact that the European Community (and, more recently, Union) has had on all walks of life are unlikely to go away. The process of integration and expansion continues and is likely to do so well into the next millennium. It is impossible to predict what the full outcome will be – a lively Federal Europe, strengthened autonomy to regional government, a disintegration of the whole concept of European integration? One thing is certain: the European Union will continue to exact a growing influence, both directly and indirectly, on local government and the way that it operates.

WORKPIECE 4.2

THE IMPACT OF THE EUROPEAN UNION

The built environment professions are being increasingly affected by the policies, programmes and legislation coming from the European Union. Give examples of how such policies are influencing the practice of the professions you are interested in. You might consider this question in relation to the following issues:

- Funding of development.
- Public procurement.
- Tendering arrangements.
- Environmental impact assessments.
- Land reclamation.
- Education and training.

The main pressures on and responses by built environment professionals in local government may be summarized as shown in Figure 4.1.

HOW THE DEVELOPMENT PROCESS IS MANAGED

The public sector in general, and in particular local government in its various forms, has an important role to play as a facilitator of development. This role is essentially concerned with the planning and financing of development.

Pressures

privatization

interagency relationships

politicization

European context

professional officer in Local Government

Responses

changing professional roles

management of the development process

collaborative practice

partnerships

Figure 4.1 Pressures on and responses of the professional officer in local government.

PLANNING

Before any development can proceed, the necessary permissions must be acquired from local authorities. Typically a planning application must be submitted which goes to committee with a recommendation. The committee, composed of local political representatives, will either grant or refuse planning permission. With the trend towards increasing politicization described earlier, it is more common for committees to overturn officer recommendations. The lobbying of local politicians becomes an important aspect of successful development planning and local politicians may become active partners in the development process.

Local authority planning officers have developed the planning brief to help to control and manage the development process. Planning briefs have been used to manage the disposal of publicly owned land or to provide a clear context for complex developments in the private sector. In essence a planning brief contains a policy statement about the use and development of land which contains an indication that the granting of permission for any development is not likely to be a problem if the proposed development accords with the constraints contained within the brief. Thus a planning brief ensures that the type of development proposed is in accordance with structure plans and local plans, for example, and acts as a facilitator of development. For the sort of complex development project that needs a partnership between public and private sectors, this type of activity at the planning stage is essential to a successful project. In addition, in return for facilitating development, local authority officers may seek 'planning gain' where community benefits may accrue as the result of any development. For example, a planning brief may indicate that a large housing development would only be accepted if community facilities were provided as part of the development.

FINANCE

Development finance, provided in one form or another by central government, is funnelled through public sector agencies. This money is often made available only if matching finance is made available from the private sector or if the community is involved in managing the project. Chapter 5 describes the emergence of modern collaborative partnerships which have developed in response to these pressures. Chapter 8 looks at a range of examples of community involvement in the development process.

Finally, because of the changing roles of members and officers in local government, political support is an important ingredient for the successful completion of any project.

WORKPIECE 4.3

THE ROLE OF THE PUBLIC SECTOR IN DEVELOPMENT PROJECTS

Consider any development project with which you are familiar and discuss the role played by the public sector by referring to the topics below:

- Obtaining permission for development.
- Seeking funding for the development.
- Professional advice.
- Lobbying of local councillors.
- Coordination between agencies and departments.
- Community involvement.

NEW PARTNERSHIPS IN COLLABORATIVE PRACTICE

As the traditional and distinctive division of roles in the development process between the public and private sector is breaking down, and professional officers are having to adapt their roles to these new circumstances, the climate has been right for a range of experiments in a new collaboration between professionals in different agencies in the public and private sector. Identifying the necessary stages within the development process itself, and building an effective team which incorporates all the skills required, has become an essential part of the process. Each development scheme may require a different combination of skills and knowledge and have a different balance of private/public sector involvement. The role of the project manager, discussed in Chapter 7, has developed to respond to this situation. Formerly many projects were managed by professional officers within the public sector; nowadays it is more likely that the project may be managed within the private sector, with the public sector acting as a facilitator of development.

This chapter has pointed to contextual shifts in the way that any development process is managed and has considered the problems and opportunities presented to professionals working in local government. (Chapter 5 deals with these themes in more detail in considering the form which these new partnerships can take.) It has explored how legislation has influenced the nature and role of the public sector and discussed emerging trends in public services. The European context has been outlined and the way in which the parliament in Brussels has established new parameters for the built environment professions has been discussed.

SUMMARY

The issues covered in the chapter are:

CHECKLIST

- the privatization of local authority roles;
- the effect of compulsory competitive tendering;
- the emergence of interagency government;
- the politicization of local government;
- how European legislation has affected local government;
- summary of the main pressures and responses by built environment professionals operating in local government;
- how the development process is managed;
- new partnerships in collaborative practice.

REFERENCES

1. Young, K. (1980) What is Local Government for?, in *Essays on the Future of Local Government* (ed. M. Goldsmith), West Yorkshire County Council.
2. Stoker, G. (1991) *The Politics of Local Government*, 2nd edn, Macmillan.
3. Newton, K. and Karran, T.J. (1985) *The Politics of Local Expenditure*, Macmillan.
4. Walsh, K. (1989) Competition and Service in Local Government, in *The Future of Local Government* (eds J. Stewart and G. Stoker), Macmillan.
5. Dunleavy, P. (1980) *Urban Political Analysis*, Macmillan.
6. Nadin, V. and Daniels, R. (1992) Consultants and Development Plans. *The Planner*, 7 August.
7. Young, K. and Davies, M. (1990) *The politics of Local Government since Widdicombe*, Joseph Rowntree Trust, York.
8. Newton, K. (1976) *Second City Politics*, Oxford University Press, Oxford.
9. Gyford, J., Leach, S. and Game, C. (1989) *The Changing Politics of Local Government*, Unwin Hyman.
10. Noel, E. (1993) *Working Together – The Institutions of the European Community*, European Documentation, Brussels.

FURTHER READING

Cochrane, A. (1993) *Whatever happened to Local Government?* Oxford University Press.

Fontaine, P. (1993) *A Citizen's Europe*, European Documentation, Brussels.

George, S. (1990) *An Awkward Partner: Britain in the European Community*, Oxford University Press.

Hogwood, B. (1992) *Trends in British Public Policy. Do Governments make any Difference?* Oxford University Press.

Isaac-Henry, K. *et al.* (1993) *Management in the Public Sector: Challenge and Change*, Chapman & Hall.

Leach, S. *et al.* (1990) *After Abolition: the operation of the post 1986 metropolitan government system in England*, Institute of Local Government (INLOGOV), University of Birmingham.

Local Goverment International Bureau (1994) *The Democratic Dimension: The European Parliament and Local Government*, London.

Stewart, J. and Stoker, G. (1989) *The Future of Local Government*, Macmillan.

Wilson, D. and Game, C. (1994) *Local Government in the United Kingdom*, Macmillan.

PARTNERSHIP IN THE DEVELOPMENT PROCESS

CHAPTER FIVE

ALAN CAVE

There have been many fundamental changes in the nature, the need for and the circumstances of partnership in the development process in the UK over the last 10 years.

This chapter seeks to identify the reasons for the increasing encouragement towards partnership on the one hand and, on the other, the increasing necessity for partnership arrangements as a prerequisite for successful development in certain circumstances. The concept of partnership in the development process is not new. However, it has now become either a prerequisite for development or a framework within which attitudes of each of the technical professions need to change and adapt.[1] This is in order to ensure that each continues to contribute effectively to the team effort involved in sustainable development.

The idea of sustainability in development, promoted by the present UK government, requires that new projects should be seen to contribute as long-term initiatives protecting the environment and involving greater energy efficiency.[2] Thus the contribution of technical specialists in the project involves greater complexity and corporate commitment than may previously have been so. Chapter 9 of this book develops further the concept of sustainability in the development process.

OBJECTIVES

After reading this chapter you should be able to:

- understand the definition of partnership, who the partners are in the development process, and the forms which such partnerships may take;

- describe the fundamental importance in the UK of urban regeneration as a process and focus for development;

- consider the implementation of partnership arrangements and the role of project team building within an increasingly complex development process;

- describe the changing role of the public sector in the development process and its potential for creating partnership opportunities.

INTRODUCTION

Underlying the changing emphasis on partnership are several important changes that have influenced the role of the partnership. Briefly, these include:

- Changes in the world economy and the UK economy and, with recession, the need for new initiatives and inducements to be found that will enable development to contribute to economic recovery.

- Government policy with an increasing emphasis upon privatization of public sector services, and the subsequent encouragement given to the substantial release of public sector land and property assets.

- Social and economic changes, including population change, which have brought about shifts in the demand for certain services (for example, levels of primary and secondary school provision) that have reduced the need for certain types of public sector land and property assets.

- The increasing emphasis upon urban regeneration as a contribution towards economic recovery. This has included new mechanisms to help both the public and private sectors, bringing together their resources towards reversing the continuous decay and decline of the older urban areas. In this process it is freely recognized by public and private sector alike, that market forces alone cannot achieve continuing physical improvements in the older areas. Substantial inducements and new mechanisms, often novel in their form, are needed to stimulate job and housing opportunities and the improvement of the environment.

● Changes in the operational needs of both public sector bodies and private sector enterprise. Increasing improvements in the effective use of floorspace and land and changes in the operation of public sector services have led to a very substantial increase in assets that need to be realized as they become surplus to requirements.

The combination of all these factors requires property professionals to rethink significantly their approaches to the provision of services and their contribution to the development process.

There is no one model definition of partnership but a prerequisite is the bringing together of two or more parties on a cooperative basis. These parties would provide an input of assets in land, finance or property terms, and could also contribute a range of skills to ensure that the best calibre of team is applied to a specific project.

Likewise, partners would look towards a share of the outputs from a scheme. These would include a return on investment, social and economic benefits arising from the projects, possible reuse of the development once completed, and the possibility of sharing in income when the scheme is in operation.

For the purposes of this chapter, partnership is not necessarily seen as a formal organizational arrangement. It could take the form of a joint venture as a joint company, in which case some form of legal agreement would be required.

The partnership may involve a developer who would take responsibility for undertaking a project but who would rely on a number of other participants by way of cooperation or grant assistance – for example, where some form of legal agreement might be required relating to the terms of financial contribution from the parties and agreement as to the sharing of outputs upon completion.

In some cases, a partnership may be a cooperative venture where the public agency (such as a central government department or a local authority) might contribute skills or advice on either a remunerative or non-remunerative basis, with the developer taking responsibility for coordinating the project and assembling appropriate technical skills.

DEFINITION OF PARTNERSHIP IN THE DEVELOPMENT PROCESS

THE PARTNERS IN THE DEVELOPMENT PROCESS

This chapter does not set out arrangements for development projects where the partners are specifically confined to the private or public sector. A private sector development project might involve a developer together with a series of financial contributors, directing a team of professionals towards scheme completion and its subsequent disposal/management.

Similarly a public sector scheme (for example, undertaken by a local authority) may involve only in-house resources, with no private sector participation. This is becoming more the exception than the rule in view of the changing role of the public sector as discussed in Chapter 4.

In general terms, over the last 10 years the UK government has looked increasingly towards private sector participation in a project as a prerequisite for funding; or it requires the demonstration of some form of partnership between the private sector and other bodies (for example, a training and enterprise council) in order for public sector funds to be made available to support a project.[3]

Typically, particularly in the field of urban regeneration, the partners in a project are likely to involve a combination of the following:

- Central government as the provider of grant aid and other forms of financial assistance towards a project based on established criteria for eligibility.
- The focus of government assistance could be the Department of the Environment through the recently established regional office framework as set up under the proposals for the Single Regeneration Budget which applied with effect from the financial year 1994/95.
- Government departments as contributors of land or property which is, or is likely to become, surplus to operational requirements and therefore available for use by other parties.
- The local authority as a landowner or formulator of policy and provider of finance or land/premises towards a project.
- The local authority as local planning authority providing a stimulus through a development plan or technical advice, or requiring to control the development through planning consent and other regulatory measures such as building regulations, environmental ratification or highway works. Technical teams could be provided depending on the nature of the scheme either as advisers or as professionals required to be involved on a remunerative basis.
- The landowner, who will contribute the land/premises to a development project.

- An urban regeneration agency such as an Urban Development Corporation, New Town Corporation or a City Challenge Enterprise. These bodies have powers to provide land, technical advice or grant aid together with provision of technical services, loans or other incentives towards development processes.
- The developer other than the landowner. The developer normally provides finance and technical coordinating expertise and possibly physical assets towards the scheme with an expectation of reasonable returns in exchange for contributing risk. Increasingly, in the context of urban regeneration, there are built-in controls on the level of profits achieved by a developer on schemes subsidized by the public sector through, for example, grant aid, where clawback provisions would ensure that the public purse shares in any excess returns beyond those anticipated at the commencement of a scheme.
- A Training and Enterprise Council, Chamber of Commerce and indeed the community, each of whom may contribute advice and encouragement or participate in the decision making leading to agreement on a development project.
- The technical team, whoever appoints them. These may include the full range of professional inputs, covering legal aspects, finance, surveying skills, engineering skills (highways, mechanical, electrical, structural, etc.), quantity surveyors, town planners, designers, landscape consultants, noise consultants, geotechnic experts and others.

The last 10 years have seen, in parallel to the shift towards partnership, a very substantial increase in the extent of public sector land and property assets becoming available to the market. This has had significant implications for the nature of partnership arrangements between public and private sectors.

An understanding of the reasons behind this increase helps in the appreciation of why partnership is increasingly significant in its own right. The changes are wide ranging and can be summarized as:

- changing user and service requirements from property, including more comprehensive and regular assessment of the estate, how it can be made more efficient and how it responds to the needs of the user;
- the growing commitment to urban regeneration;

INCREASE IN PUBLIC SECTOR ASSETS ON THE MARKET: IMPLICATIONS FOR PARTNERSHIP

- reduced government finance towards development projects in the public sector;
- increased emphasis on estate strategies in the public sector.

CHANGING USER AND SERVICE REQUIREMENTS FROM PROPERTY

The pattern of service delivery within the public sector (and recently privatized organizations) has changed markedly in recent years. These changes have applied in the higher and further education sector, secondary education, the provision of health services and energy and communications.

However, in recent years all public sector bodies have undertaken thorough assessments of their current space utilization and considered ways in which more effective use could be made of less space. In some sectors such as secondary education this has also been a result of reduced demand arising from changes in population structure.

In addition, substantial and often very complex estates have come on to the market from the energy sector as a result of improved performance in energy production together with strategic changes in the methods of production.

Whilst in some cases the public sector body has required an immediate capital receipt from freehold disposal, the realization of assets has often been achieved more through an income flow over time than through a partnership arrangement. Thus a variety of arrangements, yielding a profit share or a stream of income over a period of years, has been preferred to an outright sale. In this connection, professional teams have been required not only to establish the appropriate partnership but also to maintain a firm control of the asset once it has been developed or redeveloped to ensure effective disposal of parts and also continuing management of the new asset achieved through development or redevelopment.

The decision to retain and reuse or to redevelop can be heavily influenced by the availability of pump-priming resources. In the older inner city areas, the availability of grant aid has been able to bridge the gap, yielding profitable schemes that shift the balance towards redevelopment. City Challenge areas in older city districts are important foci for using priming resources for redevelopment which might otherwise not take place.

Newtown City Challenge in Birmingham is a good example where three 'flagship' development projects require grant aid to take off and to contribute to community needs through new jobs, homes and shopping facilities.

In this decision-making process, various technical skills are required relating to development, finance, appreciation of the market and the costing of new buildings and provision of infrastructure. Negotiation of grant aid is also an important contribution to the professional team.

It is estimated by the RICS that there are over 600 000 acres of derelict and underused land within the older urban areas that, with appropriate treatment, are capable of being recycled towards important job-creating opportunities or the provision of housing and environmental improvement.

The processes of land assembly coupled with land restoration and provision of infrastructure are key ingredients of urban regeneration initiatives which, without grant aid, would not in themselves bring about development unless there was a substantial increase in confidence and land values that would enable the land provided to be brought forward and developed.[4]

The inner cities have for too long been hampered by stagnation in the value of property and land, leading to deterioration in condition and to market interest being concentrated in other areas. The very real and deep-seated problems of industrial decline, redundancy of assets at a faster rate than economic upturn that would enable redevelopment to be effectively undertaken with speed, and the lack of any financial incentive to bring forward land have all contributed to the stagnation of these areas.

Historically, UK government strategy for the inner city has been to use grant aid to stimulate action by government-sponsored agencies and the private sector to turn land around and enable areas, after substantial regeneration, to achieve self-sustained growth without a continuing long-term need for public sector subsidy.[5] A series of agencies have, therefore, been introduced over the last 10 years in order to focus investment and to provide pump-priming mechanisms through finance or land assembly, reclamation and infrastructure. The agencies then sell on land to the development industry which would have been incapable of undertaking such action alone.

Many of these agencies have participated in partnership arrangements and assisted not only in stimulating development but also in the financing of it and assistance towards training and business arising from the development itself. Many of these Urban Development Corporations and, more recently, City Challenge enterprises have had

URBAN
REGENERATION

substantial sums of money available in order to pump prime development and encourage social and economic improvements. The Urban Development Corporations have frequently included specialist teams on their establishments but have invariably used consultants in respect of property matters, planning, feasibility studies, engineering, etc.

Each of the City Challenge enterprises, of which there are now over 30 across the UK in many of the older urban areas, has been allocated £37.5 million for a 5-year period to help to regenerate local areas. These organizations have generally employed few technical specialists and therefore such expertise has been provided either by consultants or by the local authority within whose area the enterprise is located.

A significant key characteristic of these organizations, including Urban Development Corporations, is their temporary nature since they were set up for limited periods only, in order that they could help to stimulate the process of self-regeneration, and would be wound down over a period as the key objective was achieved. Likewise, the New Town Development Corporations have been wound down as their key objectives of development stimulus have largely been completed.

The New Town corporations had responsibility for land assembly and control of land in their areas and very substantial acreages have been brought forward for development within the context of New Town master plans.

REDUCED GOVERNMENT FINANCE TOWARDS PUBLIC SECTOR DEVELOPMENT

In recent years many parts of the public sector, including local government, have received less direct financial assistance from central government towards development projects. The increasing independence and emphasis on self-financing have encouraged many such bodies to look towards the realization of assets as a means of obtaining finance for ploughing back into the provision of services.

In the Health Service, for example, the realization of land and property assets brought about through rationalization of health services has enabled resources to be recycled into service provision. There has been a significant availability of redundant hospital complexes within both the urban areas and the countryside as a result of rationalization of the provision of health services. Each of these bodies in the public sector has had certain enabling legislation to allow them to undertake partnership schemes varying in their nature and complexity.

Thus a series of opportunities has been presented for establishing partnership arrangements as long as the overall control of finance does not pass out of the public sector. The joint venture arrangement has been a very significant element of opportunity for major development projects and some case studies will be cited as examples later in this chapter.

ESTATE STRATEGIES

In recent years the government has also encouraged public sector bodies to prepare estate strategies and property audits that examine future space needs in the light of the changing requirements for land and property. As well as the health service, the universities and further education colleges have been undertaking estate strategies and reviews of the performance of the estate. One purpose of these strategies – looking at needs for, say, a 5-year period and beyond – is to justify the continuing occupation of space. They also act as a framework for obtaining further central government funding or approval to obtain resources from the money market in order for schemes to take place.

In the higher education sector and in the health service, joint schemes have been encouraged where private sector interests together with the educational or health institutions could undertake projects of mutual benefit, thus introducing private sector sponsorship into the core function of the organization.

The requirement for better utilization of space has involved inducements and also (in the case of the health service) penalty systems for the continuing retention of unoccupied or surplus space. In the private sector, the importance of the book value of property in a major firm's accounts also requires that best use is made of property: rationalization takes place where clearly surplus assets may become a liability.

All these factors have produced major new opportunities for development involving partnership arrangements.

IMPLEMENTATION OF PARTNERSHIP ARRANGEMENTS

Where public and private sector organizations seek a partnership approach to a new project, team building can involve either specialists from both organizations or a developer assembling the team on behalf of all parties. There have been very important changes in the relationships between the various professions associated with property, in recent years.

Traditionally, technical professionals tended to be either public or private sector employees and there was limited movement between the sectors from a career point of view. More recently, there has been a general increase in the interchange between the sectors with regard to property advice. Coupled with this, many public sector organizations have been obliged to privatize technical specialist teams and indeed many local authority departments have now been the subject of acquisition by private sector interests.

In addition, compulsory competitive tendering (CCT) has meant that many local authority departments compete with each other for the provision of services such that private sector acumen has inevitably had to be developed from within various professional teams.

There has also been a significant breakdown of traditional skill boundaries between the professions, resulting in increased competition between them. Many professional skills are no longer the preserve of one specific professional institution. For example, town planning services are now offered by planning consultancies, local authority departments, firms of property consultants, engineering consultancies, the architectural profession, the legal profession and accountancy as well as landscape and design consultants.

The development process itself has become more and more complex, requiring increasing specialism within the technical professions and the need for greater in-depth knowledge by each specialism. Contaminated land, for example, is a highly complex issue where strategies towards remedial action now require a combination of legal, financial, property, geotechnical, engineering, quantity surveying and planning advice, with strong relationships between the local authority (as a controller of development) and development interest. In addition, particularly in urban regeneration, the value of the development as an end product is now measured not only in financial terms but also in terms of social and economic outputs such as the number and type of jobs, training opportunities and other community gains. Fortunately, in view of the less marketable locations of the inner city, there is in the provision of grant aid reasonable allowance for profits to be made that provide inducement to the private sector to undertake development.

The technical skill of project coordination has also become a very specialist area of expertise with a number of professions that are capable of undertaking this important role in pulling together technical teams in the development process. The urban development agencies such as Urban Development Corporations have been given wide-ranging powers to undertake a series of permutations of joint venture or partnership arrangements in the development of land and property, again far removed from the straightforward disposal of land.

In recent years there has also been increasing amalgamation of technical firms with a tendency towards larger firms offering multidisciplinary skills. This has led to the demise of the medium-size independent firm.

Whilst the traditional role of local authorities as controllers of development has now been balanced by the more proactive role of providing guidance to development through the preparation of development plans and regeneration initiatives, there has in parallel been a significant increase in the amount of environmental control applying to the development process and the operation of new development. Environmental management has become a major new growth area with the need for strong energy conservation programmes, good practice guides, stringent regulations on omissions and the requirement for environmental impact assessments in many cases.

With the Environmental Protection Act of 1990 there has been a significant increase in the regulation of waste disposal as well as other forms of waste treatment. This has led to an increase in professional team requirements as well as in the stages of ratification required by developers in obtaining appropriate consents.

The growing complexity of the development process, as indicated above, has extended the technical inputs required in the development process. Local authorities, health authorities and others have found that they have insufficient demand, or indeed resources, available to contain such teams in-house. This has led to a substantial increase in the use of outside consultants by the public sector in the formulation of development projects, regardless of the involvement of the private sector as developer.

INCREASE IN REGULATIONS

There has been a very substantial decline in the availability of new dwellings in the local authority sector. This has in part been matched by the increased resources available and the encouragement of the Housing Corporation through which housing associations obtain their funds. The owner-occupation sector has been encouraged through disposal of local authority land resources and those of other public sector bodies to the private sector.

Increasing attention has been given to the provision of specialist housing not only as social housing to meet particular needs but also in the case of student accommodation. The latter area has been a good example of partnership arrangements. For example, universities have often involved the private sector in the provision of space to rent, with the university providing the guarantee of continuing student numbers to the private sector interest. Grant aid has been available for the provision of student accommodation, which has significantly assisted in such provision in the older areas, bringing people and their spending into the

REDUCTIONS IN LOCAL AUTHORITY HOUSE BUILDING

older areas as well as providing much needed accommodation close to the city or inner town universities.

THE BENEFITS OF PARTNERSHIP

A significant range of benefits have accrued as a result of partnership approaches to the development process. These benefits have included:

- Bringing together the best technical inputs towards complex projects with the best specialists appointed either by the developer or by the public sector body.
- Continuing partnership involving the public sector as, say, landowner, with continued participation in a scheme for a period. This has maintained accountability in the use of the public sector asset and yielded continuing income for ploughing back into the public sector service provision.
- Partnership has clearly stimulated the urban regeneration process and the recycling of unused and underused land, often derelict or contaminated.
- Partnership has invariably achieved an adequacy of resources that would not have been available from one party alone. Partnership can bring added skills, financial resources, speed of delivery and sustainability of development to a greater extent than one party being involved alone.
- Particularly where a local planning authority is involved as a partner, partnership can yield a greater level of consensus between the parties to enable speedy decisions to be made with one objective in mind. Whilst in the past a developer often sought to obtain a maximum scale of project yielding maximum returns, with inevitable confrontation with local planning authorities, consensus has invariably brought about speedier resolution of such issues and the avoidance of continuing confrontation through planning appeals and other mechanisms.
- By the joint involvement of parties possibly including a local planning authority, a series of community gains may well be achieved at a greater level than might otherwise be the case. These will be provided either through the developer voluntarily offering gains such as community open space, or agreement being reached through a legal agreement (a Section 106 Agreement under the Town and Country Planning Act 1990).

CASE STUDIES

The following workpieces consist of a series of case studies of partnership arrangements in redevelopment schemes. You are asked to consider each case study and discuss the nature of the partnership roles involved. In order to help you with this exercise you may wish to ask the following questions:

- What might be the benefits of an increased emphasis on partnership arrangements in UK development projects?
- What are the key characteristics of partnership arrangements in development projects?
- What roles could the public sector play in a partnership or collaborative approach to development?
- The government has identified a partnership as a requirement for funding. Who do you think are likely to be the types of partners in the development of an inner city project?
- What trends have influenced the emerging approach to partnership arrangements or collaboration in development in the UK during the last ten years?

WORKPIECE 5.1

CASE STUDY: REDEVELOPMENT OF REDUNDANT RACECOURSE

ISSUE To redevelop an outdated and under-utilized racecourse lying in the Green Belt but adjacent to a large conurbation.

OUTPUT A redeveloped racecourse providing grass and all-weather racing facilities; 200+ jobs in training, catering, etc.; community facilities; hotel and 30 acres (12 ha) of residential development as a pump primer towards racecourse renewal. A funding arrangement including grant aid towards £12 million scheme.

ROLES PLAYED Client (as owner) leading team.

STAGE 1
- Combination of in-house design skills, residential agency, town planning consultancy and grant aid advice.
- DOE at national and regional levels in respect of grant assessment and justification including consultant as grant appraiser.
- Local authority as Planning Authority, education and community service agency.

- City Challenge enterprise as promoter and source of finance assistance.
- Training and Enterprise Council as promoter and assistance in respect of training etc.
- Quantity surveyors in respect of scheme costing.

STAGE 2 Scheme development under quantity surveyor coordination and including design, engineering and landscape input.

COMMENTARY ON OUTCOME Scheme recognized as a flagship under a City Challenge scheme with consensus effort to achieve early redevelopment.

Local planning authority allocated 30 acres (12 ha) of the site for housing and remainder for racecourse redevelopment in the Unitary Development Plan with very little objection. Planning consent subsequently received.

DOE approved major City Grant allocation.

Scheme inception to completion covered a 12-month period in 1992/93. First race meeting attracted double previous best attendance. Private sector involvement through hotel and catering services. Training jobs and other indirect employment achieved as projected.

WORKPIECE 5.2

CASE STUDY: REDEVELOPMENT OF REDUNDANT HOSPITAL SITE 1

ISSUE   Reuse of redundant 80 acres (32 ha) Green Belt hospital with 400 000 square feet (37 000 m²) of floorspace including listed building.

OBJECTIVES
- To develop the site for 700 dwellings through refurbishment and new building to include community provision, shops and open space and new infrastructure including a spine road.
- To dispose of the site as patient service withdrawal is completed in 1995.
- To recycle sales receipts into improved health care within alternative accommodation.

ROLES   Regional Health Authority as client.

Consultancy team (external) included planning consultancy, residential and commercial agency surveyors, architects, highway and drainage teams.

Local planning authority resolved to grant planning consent subject to a legal agreement on open space, roads and phasing.

COMMENTARY ON OUTCOME   Secretary of State approved principle of development in Structure Plan as an 'exceptional circumstance' in the Green Belt. Site included in Local Plan by District Council and planning consent granted subject to legal agreements.

Site marketed to attract a developer as a partner prepared to contribute to initial infrastructure costs (no Health Service resources available to undertake pump-priming works).

Legal agreement sought to ensure refurbishment of listed buildings undertaken in parallel with new building.

WORKPIECE 5.3

CASE STUDY: REDEVELOPMENT OF REDUNDANT HOSPITAL SITE 2

ISSUE   Surplus 40 acres (16 ha) Green Belt hospital including a listed building with limited access for future commercial development.

OBJECTIVES
- To reuse the listed building and other buildings in sound condition and to redevelop others for B1 office use.
- To dispose of the complex and recycle sales receipts into patient care.
- To consider a joint venture working arrangement combining developer expertise and finance and Health Service land and property.

ROLES   Consultant team appointed to work to project coordination by the developer and Health Authority. Team included planning, design, landscape and highway advice plus legal advice in formulating the legal agreement to enable planning consent to be granted.

Local planning authority (LPA) in preparing a development brief.

Conservation consultants appointed by LPA to advise upon the treatment of the listed building and its immediate environment.

County Council in ratifying a Section 278 agreement in respect of the developer funding highway works.

COMMENTARY ON OUTCOME   Site marketed for Green Belt uses with no declared interest. Health Service arranged a joint venture by contributing land and property to the agreement and the developer providing development finance, expertise and construction. Site subject of a planning brief and subsequent application for 135 000 square feet (12 500 m²) B1 office and light industrial use.

Inclusion of site in Local Plan. Negotiation of planning consent and subsequent revisions to the scheme. Negotiations upon a Section 106 legal agreement in respect of important landscape enhancement and management, highways and phasing. Negotiations also with adjacent landowner on improved access and with County Council on highway improvements.

Planning consent granted and scheme commenced.

CASE STUDY: CITY CENTRE SHOPPING REDEVELOPMENT

ISSUE Redevelopment of outmoded retail store and adjacent land.

OBJECTIVE To construct 150 000 square feet (14 000 m²) of office floorspace, plus 30 000 square feet (2800 m²) of shops with an emphasis on energy efficient building techniques.

ROLES Investor acquired site and guided scheme from inception to disposal. Chartered Surveyors acted as project coordinators. Team included architect, mechanical, electrical and structural engineers, quantity surveyors, building surveyors and contractors.

Local planning authority advised upon planning, design and highway issues.

Chartered Surveyors advised on acquisition, concept and letting of completed floorspace.

COMMENTARY ON OUTCOME This £100 million project illustrates the range of technical inputs required for a complex development completed within 2 years of inception and fully let.

The scheme has received awards for energy efficiency.

SUMMARY

The following points may be noted:

- There is no one model approach to a partnership arrangement.
- The outcome of a development project often differs significantly from the initial objective at the start of discussions leading to a decision to undertake development. Both economic circumstances and other factors dictate the need for flexibility and adaptability of the various parties towards continuing successful partnership in the development process.
- The total commitment of the partners to a particular scheme can be instrumental in achieving output within the time originally agreed and at cost.
- Partnership or cooperation may take a variety of forms. It must be remembered that the public sector is constrained by statute in respect of the scope it possesses for undertaking certain forms of joint venture.
- The process of urban regeneration has been a major context for partnership schemes, needing flexibility and adaptability of attitude by all parties. A particular characteristic of the inner cities is the inability of the market to perform in isolation to achieve new development. Thus the urban regeneration agency acts as a critical pump primer with the stimulus of grant aid and other financial mechanisms to enable a development to become sufficiently remunerative to make it worth undertaking.
- The coordination of a development project is critical to its success and requires a particular skill and commitment.

CHECKLIST

The issues covered in the chapter are:

- definition of partnership in the development process;
- the partners in the development process;
- the reasons for the increase in public sector assets on the market and implications for partnership;
- changing user and service requirements from property;
- the centrality of the urban regeneration process;
- reduced government finance towards development by the public sector;
- estate strategies;
- implementing of partnership arrangements;
- increase in regulations;
- reductions in local authority housing building;
- the benefits of partnerships.

REFERENCES

1. Low, C.M. (1988) Public–private partnership in urban revitalisation in Britain. *Regional Studies* **22**(5) 446–51.
2. Elkin, T. and McClaren, M. (1991) *Reviving the City: Towards sustainable urban development*, Friends of the Earth/Policy Studies Institute, London.
3. Department of the Environment (1987) *Action for Cities: Building on Initative*, HMSO.
4. Healey, P. *et al.* (1992) *Rebuilding the City: Property led urban regeneration*, E & FN Spon.
5. Deakin, N. and Edwards, J. (1993) *The Enterprise Culture and the Inner City*, Routledge.

FURTHER READING

Berry, J. *et al.* (1993) *Urban Regeneration. Property and Development*, E & FN Spon.
Haughton, G. and Whitney, D. (1989) Equal Urban Partners? *The Planner*, December.
Jacobs, M. (1990) *Sustainable Development: Greening the Economy*, Fabian Society, London.

AN INTRODUCTION TO THE DESIGN/BUILD METHOD

CHRIS ARNISON

THEME

The emergence of the design/build method of construction is considered as an alternative to the traditional building process and has involved changes in the methods of building procurement and the respective roles of professionals concerned with the development process. This chapter considers in some detail the changes that have occurred in the stages of the building process.

OBJECTIVES

After reading this chapter you should be able to:

- understand the nature of the traditional building process;

- know what is meant by the design/build method of building and construction;

- be familiar with the shortcomings of the traditional method and the reasons for the emergence of design/build.

INTRODUCTION

In this chapter we shall examine the origin of the 'design and build' approach, which developed from the 'package deal' method of procuring buildings referred to in Chapter 1. We shall consider its advantages and disadvantages in the light of the experience of the past 25 years. This will involve an analysis of the roles taken by the professional 'players' in the traditional procedure for achieving a completed building, prior to the introduction of design/build, and will also critically examine the procedure itself.

THE TRADITIONAL BUILDING PROCESS

In order to understand the advantages and disadvantages of the design/build process, we must first be aware of the traditional processes. The traditional procedure, used for the majority of building projects before around 1970, was roughly as follows.

INITIAL STAGES

1. Someone – either an individual or an organization ('the client') – decides that a new building is needed.
2. The client approaches an architect and describes what is needed in as much detail as possible.
3. The architect uses this 'brief' to create a preliminary design, which is referred back to the client for comment and approval.
4. An initial estimate of cost is made.

DETAILED DESIGN STAGE

1. When the client has agreed the design concept and the approximate cost, the architect draws up plans which are submitted to the local authority for planning permission.
2. On the granting of planning permission, the architect produces detailed plans and specifications. This will require the architect to engage the services of specialists such as structural, electrical and mechanical engineers.
3. The detailed plans and specifications are sent to a quantity surveyor who will use them to produce a bill of quantities. This is a complete analysis of all the components and materials and the labour required to convert the architect's plans into a completed building.

TENDER STAGE

1. The architect sends copies of the plans and the bill of quantities to selected builders, inviting them to tender for the work. A standard form of contract will be included with the invitation to tender so that the builders are all working on the same assumptions.
2. The client and the architect will consider all the tenders received and will accept the one that they feel represents the best value for money. This is not necessarily the lowest figure, as factors such as reputation, special skills and financial standing will also be taken into account.

CONTRACT STAGE

1. A formal contract will be entered into with the successful tenderer and work will commence.

2. The architect will supervise the work through to completion and will be responsible for authorizing any variations from the initial plans and specifications which may have to be made during the work. The architect will also authorize periodic payments to the contractor based on the amount of work completed.

3. After the building is completed there will be a period of 12 months during which the building is monitored for defects. The contractor will be responsible for and bear the cost of 'snagging' (making good small defects).

4. At the end of this period, a final detailed inspection will be made by the architect, who will list any outstanding defects or uncompleted work. When these have been dealt with, the architect certifies that the building contract has been fully discharged and authorizes the last payment to the contractor of the 'retention' money (usually 5% of the total contract sum).

5. The architect remains legally responsible for the quality of both the design and the construction of the building for many years afterwards.

WORKPIECE 6.I

CASE STUDY: OFFICE DEVELOPMENT

Imagine that ABC plc has engaged the D&E Architects Partnership to solve their headquarters office problem. ABC want 500 m^2 of high quality premises on a site adjoining their main factory, with lifts to all upper floors, full air-conditioning and secure basement car park. D&E engage F&G as structural engineers, H&I as heating and ventilating consultants and J&K as mechanical engineers. The building contract is given to L&M builders, based on a bill of quantities prepared by N&O, Chartered Quantity Surveyors.

Now try to work out the following:

1. When they eventually move in, ABC find that the heating is not effective. H&I claim that they have only put in what the bill of quantities specified. What are the legal responsibilities which will have to be proved for ABC to get effective heating?

2. Draw a diagram showing all the contractual relationships in the project.

3. Assuming that the various parties' own offices are on average 15 miles apart, and a total of 30 meetings are required throughout the construction period, what will be the cost of the necessary consultations? Who pays this cost?

The central role of the architect, both as designer and as project manager, is very clear. As Workpiece 6.1 shows, there are many separate legal relationships as well as a complicated network of professional roles (Figure 6.1).

In the UK there was a post-war building boom which lasted from about 1957, when restrictions on the use of building materials were lifted, to

DISADVANTAGES OF THE TRADITIONAL PROCESS

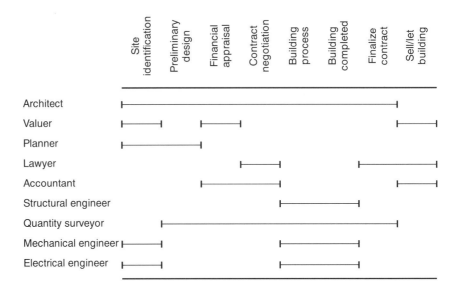

Figure 6.1 Professional roles in building construction and development.

the late 1960s. During this period it became apparent to many people that the traditional process suffered from some important disadvantages:

● The process was slow and completion dates were difficult to predict accurately.

● There was no incentive for any of the professionals to reduce costs as their fees were based on a fixed percentage of costs incurred.

● The complex interaction of professional roles made it difficult in many cases to pin responsibility for delays or mistakes on any individual member of the 'team'.

● Thus there were many legal disputes which were themselves time-consuming and expensive.

● Total costs were often well above the predicted figures because of interest charges incurred through delays and because all authorized variations during the contract carried full additional costs to the client.

THE NEED FOR CHANGE

To those clients for whom speed of building, accuracy of predicted cost and economy were of prime importance, the disadvantages clearly outweighed the advantages of continuing with a traditional process in which great emphasis was placed on creative design and on long-established professional relationships. Such clients were largely in the commercial development field dealing with office and industrial buildings, shopping centres, car parks and the like. For them two prime objectives were speed of construction (so that market opportunities could be grasped while a demand existed) and fixed costs (so that projects could be accurately evaluated in advance on very competitive profit margins).

It is not surprising, therefore, that in response to such a demand the larger construction companies, who already employed architects, engineers and quantity surveyors as full-time salaried staff, should offer a simple comprehensive service. They could, and did, offer to design and build whatever the client wanted, from start to finish and at a fixed price, with a fixed completion date.

The advantages have been summarized as:

ADVANTAGES OF DESIGN/BUILD

- single responsibility;
- speed of building;
- financial control;
- completion on time;
- economic building;
- client relationships.

SINGLE RESPONSIBILITY   Whatever the problem, failure or defect that might arise, the contractor is solely responsible and has no way of 'passing the buck'.

SPEED OF BUILDING   Where the various operations are being carried out in-house by an integrated team of designers and builders, the contractor has maximum opportunity to reduce communication delays, to overlap operations and to offer a faster approach to building.

FINANCIAL CONTROL   Most organizations work within very tight budgets, with fixed amounts for approved building projects. Development projects usually have a known maximum expenditure if they are to be viable (i.e. produce an acceptable profit margin). Before a contract is signed the contractor agrees with the client on a fixed contract price which can only be varied by the client's own further instructions. All other expenses and costs are included in the contract sum.

COMPLETION ON TIME   There are many projects where 'overrun' will be very damaging to the client, particularly for commercial and industrial buildings. Close collaboration at the design stage within an in-house design and building team ensures that the design has 'buildability' (i.e. is relatively easy actually to construct), that only efficient sub-contractors are used, that long-delivery materials which are known to be in short supply are ordered in advance and that unnecessarily complex detailing is eliminated. This enables contractors to give realistic fixed completion dates with confidence and without having to add large margins to their quoted fixed prices to cover themselves.

ECONOMIC BUILDING The various time savings and the reduction in the frustrating and inefficient communications problems outlined above all lead towards lower costs because the overall time-scale is reduced and the building is uncomplicated. Design costs are, of course, included in the lump sum tender price, but as a result of the close integration the total man hours of the team are less than would be required in the traditional system and these savings can be reflected in the price. Furthermore, with faster building both the client's and the contractor's financing charges are reduced and the building becomes operational sooner, producing an earlier return on the client's capital outlay.

CLIENT RELATIONSHIPS The contractor and client are in close contact from inception to completion of a project. This enables the contractor to understand more fully the functional requirements that the building has to satisfy and to ensure that they are met.[1]

Research carried out by *Building* magazine[2] in mid 1993 clearly indicated that clients agreed broadly with the above summary. Sixty per cent of the respondents believed that design/build can save money over other ways of procuring buildings and over half believed that there are significant time savings through improved coordination and fewer project conflicts. Respondents stated that some 20% of their future projects would utilize the design/build approach; at present the figure is about 10%. These last figures do, of course, put the significance of design/build in context: at present nine out of ten new buildings do not use it, and in ten years time eight out of ten will still not use it. If the advantages set out above are in fact real, why do not all clients use design/build? To understand this we must consider in more detail the commercial and professional relationships and roles in the traditional process.

QUALITY CONTROL   The chief merit which has always been claimed for the traditional architect-managed process is a high level of quality control exercised on behalf of the client. Both design quality and execution quality are enhanced when a single highly trained professional has overall control of all the parties in the process.

THE CONTRACTUAL DOCUMENTATION   This has been refined and elaborated over many years and thoroughly tested in the courts; it provides strong but flexible protection to the client. Standard JCT (Joint Construction Tribunal) contracts in which the central role of the architect is explicitly stated are widely understood throughout the construction industry. They make provision for controlling and, where necessary, replacing both subcontractors and professional consultants. Where disputes arise there are well established procedures for resolving them through the process of arbitration, which is cheaper and quicker than court action.

SAVING MONEY   Money is saved by preparing one detailed set of plans and contract documents in the office of the client's architect and then sending them to a number of selected tenderers. Where a client needs to decide to which of several possible design/build contractors the project should be entrusted, they all have to do a great deal of initial design and costing work which will inevitably be abortive for all but one of them. The cost of such abortive work must be recovered through the jobs in which they are successful.

SPECIALIST/CLIENT CONTACT   Few clients really do know exactly what they either want or need. The rest are greatly helped by being able to develop their own understanding of their needs and of the possible solutions through discussion with a trained creative designer, and of participating in the process of working general ideas up into detailed plans. Many corporate clients feel more at home 'brain-storming' in a group of specialists than setting out their needs in a traditional written brief, and design/build teams are well suited to answer such a need. Such meetings also develop personal bonds between the team and the client which are of great value during the remainder of their working relationship.

Over the 25 years during which design/build has been developing, two distinct varieties of the genre have emerged. They have been described

ADVANTAGES OF THE TRADITIONAL PROCESS

Learning Resources Centre

THE PRESENT POSITION

87

by Janssens[3] as either employer-led or contractor-led. In effect they represent two extremes of a series of variations (Figure 6.2) where the most employer-led form is the Develop and Construct type at the top of the left-hand column and the most contractor-led is the Turnkey type at the bottom of the right-hand column. Which form is finally adopted will depend on the type of building that is proposed and (except where the building is either quite simple or of a type that the client has commissioned several times before) on the results of an initial feasibility study.

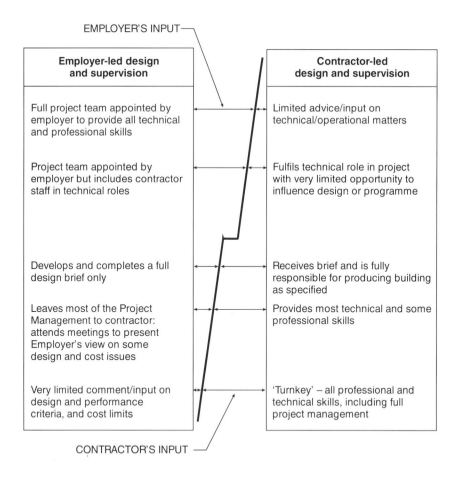

Figure 6.2 Variations in design/build projects. (Adapted from[3].)

Feasibility studies are strongly advocated by the Chartered Institute of Building (CIOB)[1] as a necessary preliminary stage which can save much time and expense. Such studies will normally be carried out by independent consultants, though large organizations such as national retailers or manufacturers may find it economic to employ in-house teams. Each study will cover:

- an objective assessment of the optimum size, shape and type of building required, including site characteristics such as gradient, geology and space for future expansion;
- local planning policy and history;
- availability of essential services, with particular reference to effluent disposal;
- site history to identify previous uses and the likelihood of site contamination or of old services or underground structures;
- an assessment of the approximate cost and time-scale for the proposed project.

Assuming that a feasibility study is favourable the client next decides on the type of design/build which best suits the particular project and will prepare a detailed client's brief. This is one of the most important elements of a successful project and is examined in detail below.

Prior to sending out the detailed brief, most clients wish to select lists of contractors with whom they are willing to deal. Such 'preselection' is based on knowledge of the experience, resources and competence of a wide range of contractors and will have regard to the character, size location and time constraints of the particular project. Clients who regularly commission design/build, or indeed traditional building projects, will regularly monitor and update a list of approved contractors.

For many clients the financial resources and stability of a contractor are critical considerations and in recent years have outweighed other qualities such as staff expertise and proven team-working skills. This is because of the high cost of concluding a project where the main contractor has failed financially. It has led, in the writer's own experience, to clients paying at least as much attention to contractors' internal accounting and cost control systems as to their site management and supervision skills. Virtually all contractors offering a design/build service produce promotional literature which is circulated widely to potential clients. Where such literature attracts the attention of a client it is usual for representatives of the contractor's design/build team to be interviewed (the so-called 'beauty parade') and to take the client on a tour of completed projects before being included on the client's approved contractor list.

THE CLIENT'S BRIEF

It hardly needs saying that the greater the detail in the client's brief, the more accurately will the contractor interpret the client's needs and the more precise will be the price quoted. But briefs which precisely specify the shape, layout, services or materials of a building detract from the contractor's overall responsibility for design. Wherever practical the brief should limit itself to statements of function and performance standards, though these should themselves be very detailed. The requirements should be set out in a way which leaves the designers with maximum scope to use their initiative and experience to offer optimum solutions. The CIOB's guidance note[1] puts the position in these terms:

> In undertaking the design of a building to satisfy a client's brief, it is vital that contractors accept their responsibilities in terms of its interpretation. A brief cannot be fully explicit. Complying with an item in the brief will have implications which are not stated. The contractor's designers are expected to have both experience and knowledge to anticipate the additional works implicit in the brief and include them in their design. Where not included the client would be justified in demanding their inclusion at no extra cost. For example, certain industrial organizations require that vehicles delivering materials or collecting goods are brought inside the factory premises at work floor level. The designer must anticipate the situation when vehicles arrive with snow on them which melts on to the work floor. Suitable means of draining the floor must be allowed for and included even if not specified in the brief.

The content of the brief should be as follows:

● Details of client, including identity of parent or holding company where applicable, nature and size of business or activity carried on and name and telephone number of person to contact.
● List of documents included with or forming part of the brief.
● An agreed period of notice to submit a tender, date for submission, period for acceptance and arrangements for notification of successful and unsuccessful tenderers.
● Number of firms invited to tender.
● List of consultants who have been involved in drawing up the brief and their intended involvement in later stages of the project. In

particular, the present position as regards planning consents should be fully stated.

It should be noted that the use of the design/build method does not remove the client's opportunity to seek competitively priced services or products. It is common for clients to approach a number of possible design/build contractors and to invite them to compete for the work by putting forward, at their own expense, proposals based on a preliminary design brief. However, the majority of clients recognize that such a process inevitably adds to the total cost and prefer to produce a detailed design brief which is then submitted to one contractor who formally confirms agreement to tender within a specified time.

WORKPIECE 6.2

EXAMPLE OF A CLIENT'S BRIEF

Draft an outline of a brief from a private school to a local building contractor for the conversion of a large barn into a gymnasium and the construction of an open-air swimming-pool on land adjoining the barn, with new changing rooms for pupils and staff.

In the event of a brief being sent to a number of selected tenderers they will all wish to visit the site and to check the information received very carefully. This may result in requests for additional information, which should be provided to all the tenderers at the same time and in the same form.

Where a detailed design brief is provided the tenderer must now go through the whole process of detailed design in order that accurate costings can be made on which to base the proposal. As indicated above, this involves much more work than is required for the preparation of a traditional building tender where full drawings and a specification have already been prepared. Teamwork in the tendering contractor's offices is of crucial importance in keeping such costs down and in producing a 'buildable' proposal at a competitive price. The three main elements of the construction process – designers, estimators and construction managers – must work as a unified team so that the cost implications of a particular design idea are appreciated immediately, along with any operational problems that may be encountered in actually realizing the design on site. Contractors specializing in design/build work will each have developed a tender preparation procedure that best suits their particular staff and corporate ethos, but all such procedures will need to cover the following points:

- The role of coordinator or team leader is of prime importance. This individual carries the responsibility for programming the sequence of events which must take place before a firm price can be put forward to the client, and of ensuring that deadlines are met and, where necessary, sanctions are applied to those failing to meet them.

- The various operations necessary to produce a tender are highly interdependent, so that frequent consultation between the team members – structural engineer, planning consultant, landscape architect, mechanical engineer, interior designer, etc. – is essential. Efficient circulation of memos of meetings or discussions, and particularly of decisions, must take place.

- The final tender price will be based on the professional team's work but may be either higher or lower depending on purely commercial considerations such as the known budget of the client, financial risk and anticipated changes in interest rates.

SUMMARY

Design/build is a good example of interprofessional collaboration at work in a very competitive and commercial context.

It is characterized by a clear shift from the old professional boundaries of the past, with their inevitable inefficiencies and delays, to a strongly team-oriented approach in which technical and professional training provide expertise but not authority.

Leadership in a design/build team falls on the person most suited to it and may move from one member of the team to another at different stages in a project.

Design/build projects often make use of prefabricated or standard components but are equally capable of producing original and inventive design solutions to a client's needs in which the client has played an active part.

Since the concept of design/build was first introduced more than 25 years ago the emphasis has shifted from merely achieving speed and cheapness to a real concern for the right balance of design quality and production efficiency.

CHECKLIST

The issues covered in this chapter are:

- **the traditional building process;**

- the need for change;
- advantages of design/build;
- advantages of the traditional process;
- the present position;
- feasibility studies;
- the client's brief.

REFERENCES

1. CIOB (1988) Design and Build, Code of Estimating Practice, Supplement No. 2.
2. CIOB (1993) Design and Build. Supplement to Building, 30 July.
3. Janssens, D. (1992) Design Build Explained, McMillan, London.

FURTHER READING

CIOB (1993) Space Race – Managing Design and Build. *Chartered Builder*, October.

Property Week (1994) The Great D and B debate. *Property Week*, 25 August.

RICS (1994) *Design and Build: Trojan Horse or Gift Horse for the Quantity Surveying Consultancy*, March.

CHAPTER SEVEN

AN INTRODUCTION TO PROJECT MANAGEMENT

STEVE McCABE

THEME

What are the key new and emerging areas of work which are coming about as a result of the growth of interprofessional activities? What impact do they have on the nature of the development process and the way in which the professions interact? Project management is viewed as a way of achieving success in the attainment of objectives. These objectives are determined by the end result – the project. The usual requirement in completing a building project is to put together materials, labour, plant and money in such a way as to ensure that the end result is correct. For clients this means that the finished product must be in accordance with their wishes, which are set out in drawings and specifications, and, crucially, it must be on time and at the desired cost. Using workpieces and examples, this chapter explores the reasons for the emergence of project management as a discipline and identifies what roles project management will fill in the future. Management skills for built environment professionals are also dealt with in Book 3 in this series (*Management and Business Skills in the Built Environment*).

OBJECTIVES

After reading this chapter you should be able to:

● know what is meant by the term 'project management';

● understand why this role came about;

● appreciate the importance of the role of project managers and their relationship with other parties in the construction process;

- identify the skills required by a project manager;

- think about the way in which the role of project management can assist in the future in terms of:
  - developing multidisciplinarity;
  - achieving harmony among project participants;
  - increasing coordination;
  - being able to provide solutions to increasingly complex problems.

INTRODUCTION

In this section we will discuss the historical context of the role of project management. As you may already appreciate, it is increasingly important and is often held in high esteem.

You will be expected to understand:

- historically, why this role has come into being;
- the limitations of the so-called traditional method of managing construction;
- what project management can achieve.

The management of construction projects is not a new phenomenon. Look around you when you visit old towns and city centres. There will usually be buildings or structures dating back at least 100 years and often many centuries. The way in which these buildings were constructed is more usually remembered for the skill of the craftsmen than the method by which they were managed. Some individuals are remembered for their innovation and vision – for example, Brunel and Wren.

THE EMERGENCE OF PROJECT MANAGEMENT

We have already discussed some of the historical background to built environment professionals (Chapters 1 and 3) but it is worth considering further the specific context of project management. The history of divisions within the professions in the construction industry is one which goes back to the feudal building guilds of the Middle Ages. The Napoleonic wars encouraged recognition of the need for large, state-led developments in France and consequently the way in which the organization of construction occurred. The result was larger-scale contractors who on the whole carried out the work in its entirety. Indeed these contractors eventually became so successful that they operated internationally, building railways in Europe, America and Asia. But it is important to remember that, traditionally, the leader of a project was the architect –

the client's representative who would provide designs for the work and administrate the building contract.

Ball[1] notes that the way in which the various professions originated has led to some of the problems the industry has experienced because of their 'rigid formalization' and 'separation from building contractors'. Generally professions were formed with the aim of protecting clients' interests. This led to the traditional form of management shown in Figure 7.1, from which you can see that there are clearly defined relationships which are either contractual or managerial.

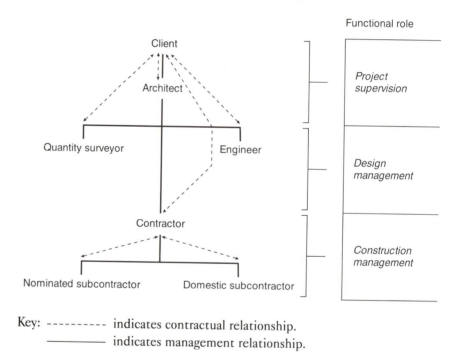

Key: - - - - - - - - indicates contractual relationship.
———————— indicates management relationship.

Figure 7.1 Traditional management structure of a project. (Source: Chartered Institute of Building (1982) *Project Management in Building*, CIOB, p. 8.)

This organization was believed to be effective for controlling projects and existed in the conventional format until, during the 1970s, there was a rapid decline in the workload of the construction industry due to massive cuts in government spending. The year 1973 is regarded as important in this context: construction was at an all-time high, it was the end of the post-war boom and construction projects were becoming increasingly complex and large. In addition, alternative forms of contract were developed.

As mentioned in Chapter 6, traditional contracting does have advantages for clients:

- They have direct control.
- They have advice from different experts.
- They can make changes during the project.

Against these are disadvantages:

- Actual production is in the control of the contractor.
- Coordination of practices is difficult.
- Relationships are prone to become 'adversarial'.
- Costs are difficult to pre-estimate and control.

There have been various studies on the need for change and it is worth looking at two quotations which summarize the widespread criticism of the traditional way of carrying out construction projects:

> The conditions which then develop on-site have often been likened to a jungle. Indeed, the average jungle may well be more orderly. At worst, site operations may be nothing less than anarchy. While it would be wrong to suggest that all building operations are conducted in such conditions the possibility of their developing is far from remote in some circumstances.[2]

> At the present time the roles in the building industry are in a state of considerable confusion. The implications of this for the experience of any individual in the building team are, firstly, he [*sic*] finds that there is no settled and stable definition of what his job actually is, and secondly, nobody else can be clear about exactly what he does and what he is responsible for without finding out a lot more about the sort of building team he is in.[3]

As a result of the inherent problems identified here, new methods emerged to deal with them. These were most notably management contracting, design and construction, and project management. We are interested in the last of these (Figure 7.2).

As Hillebrandt *et al.*[4] indicated, project management becomes necessary when projects:

- are of high value;
- are short in time-scale;
- are high in complexity;
- are novel in design or technique of construction;
- have special resource usage;
- require expertise from various participants.

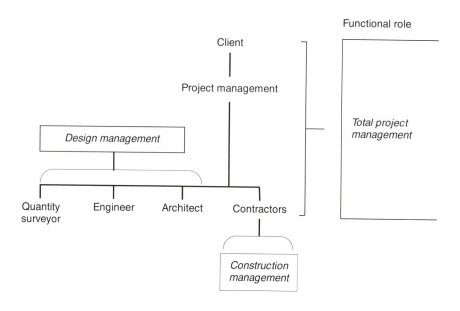

Figure 7.2 Management structure for executive project management. Functional roles are in italics. (Source: Chartered Institute of Building (1982) *Project Management in Building*, CIOB, p. 11.)

WORKPIECE 7.1

TRADITIONAL AND PROJECT MANAGEMENT

Describe the main differences between the so-called traditional form of management and project management from a client's point of view.

Which is better, and why?

WHAT IS PROJECT MANAGEMENT?

There are various definitions of project management and a useful one put forward by Walker[5] summarizes the role in its entirety:

> The planning, control and coordination of a project from conception to completion (including commissioning) on behalf of a client. It is concerned with the identification of the client's objectives in terms of utility, function, quality, time and cost, and the establishment of relationships between resources. The integration, monitoring and control of the contributors to the project

and their output, and the evaluation and selection of alternatives in pursuit of the client's satisfaction with the project outcome are fundamental aspects of construction project management.

You should be aware of the somewhat clinical nature of this definition and that whilst it is important to focus on the project it is equally important to focus on people. Barnes of the Association of Project Managers thinks that a project manager must have 'certain core skills' and with these 'should be able to tackle any project'.[6]

It is often the case that a project is regarded as being 'one off'. This implies that it will never be repeated. Recent examples might include the Channel Tunnel and the International Convention Centre in Birmingham.

Project managers are expected to have vision, so that they can put the entire scope of works into context. This requires the ability to:

- define what can be done, and how fast and for how much money;
- relay this information back to the client in order to make rational decisions;
- assemble a team of professionals to produce the relevant information;
- motivate those involved, including all those on site, to achieve the client's criteria.

The last of these abilities is particularly important: effective communication is essential for good project management. This skill, which is required in any manager, is the ability to translate the requirements of the client (usually verbal) into drawings and specifications. These will be prepared by architects, engineers and quantity surveyors, who will have been appointed for their given task probably because they are regarded as being experts and capable of achieving success and working within a close professional team.

But it must be remembered that real success is judged by the end result – the finished building. This is achieved by the contractor, who will use specialist subcontractors and suppliers. The result of using many parties with possibly differing objectives may be conflict. Good project management is about reducing the sort of problems which were identified as being typical of the traditional way of construction.

WHAT ARE THE CORE SKILLS?

WORKPIECE 7.2

PROJECT MANAGEMENT SKILLS

List the skills you feel are necessary for project management.
How do you think these can be enhanced within a project team?

WHY DOES PROJECT MANAGEMENT CONSTITUTE A DIFFERENT APPROACH?

INFLUENCES ON THE ORGANIZATION STRUCTURE

Different ways of organizing work are described below in the section about types of project management structure. The method that is selected is dependent upon many factors. The objective is to ensure that structure of the organization helps to improve the performance of the project.

According to Walker,[5] the main factors that influence the decision of how to organize the work are:

- behavioural responses;
- techniques and technology;
- decision making.

These are shown in Figure 7.3 and it can be seen that they are both interrelated and interdependent.

It is also important to note that external influences, such as economics, legislation and political considerations, play a large part in determining the success of the project.

BEHAVIOURAL RESPONSES These are the ways in which individual members of the project team interrelate with one another. Much will depend upon their attitude, which is influenced by motivation, status, personal goals and the importance that they attach to the project.

It is accepted that certain professions or particular types of contractor have strong allegiances and preformed ideas. Good project management is about reducing any potential conflict and at the same time drawing upon existing strengths.

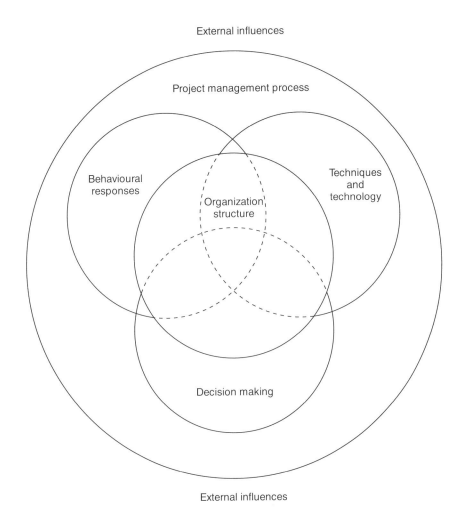

Figure 7.3 Factors in the project management process. (Source: Walker,[5] p.14.)

TECHNIQUES AND TECHNOLOGY   These are the methods used by the members of the team in order to achieve what they do. Why they do what they do will be influenced by:

● what is available at the time;
● the skills they possess;
● the need to achieve a particular outcome, e.g. speed.

The skill required by a project manager is to enhance the expertise that the various parties and individuals bring to the project. The ways in which this can be achieved will take into consideration:

● evaluation;

- appraisal;
- control methods;
- contractual obligations;
- way of dealing with design;
- how to achieve the most efficient production.

DECISION MAKING   The organizational structure must try to reflect the need for efficient and productive decision making. Much of what occurs will be as a result of the way in which the key members of the team are able to contribute. Thus, decision making should be as much as possible a result of consensus among the project teams. Ultimately the project manager, who remains accountable to the client, will have to take the final decision.

WORKPIECE 7.3

ORGANIZATIONAL STRUCTURES

What are the three main influences on the way that an organizational structure for project management will occur?

TYPES OF PROJECT MANAGEMENT STRUCTURE

It is important to be aware that project organization is often described as 'matrix management'. A simple definition[7] of a matrix is a situation in which something originates, takes form or is enclosed. This is typical of a project that is required for very special reasons. A traditional management structure – which is hierarchical (long chain of command) – is replaced by one with lateral management, bringing together vertical functional roles with the objectives of engendering team work and integration.

The project's objectives are the primary consideration, but in attempting to achieve these the organizational structure must be appropriate. The successes will often be strongly influenced by the ability of those involved in the project team to break their traditional ties and allegiances to specialist groups. Instead their effort is fully dedicated to the project.

Hamilton[8] identified types of project structure. These are:

- functional matrix;
- balanced matrix;
- project matrix;
- project team.

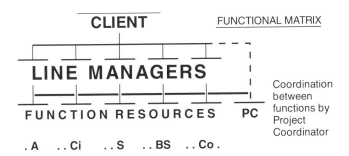

Figure 7.4 Organizational structure: functional matrix. Key: A = architecture; BS = building services; Ci = civil engineering; Co = construction; PC = project coordination; S = structural engineering.

FUNCTIONAL MATRIX This is where the project manager coordinates the 'key players' and is thus often referred to as a project coordinator (Figure 7.4).

BALANCED MATRIX In this the project manager and his/her team have equal authority with the other functional managers (Figure 7.5).

PROJECT MATRIX This is the most common of the organizational structures (Figure 7.6), in which the project manager has primary responsibility. Functional staff or firms of specialists are brought in as necessary.

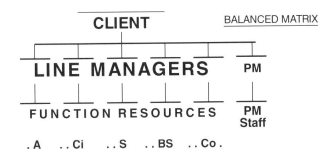

Figure 7.5 Organizational structure: balanced matrix. Key: A = architecture; BS = building services; Ci = civil engineering; Co = construction; PM = project manager; S = structural engineering.

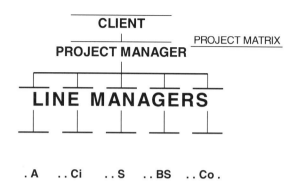

Figure 7.6 Project management: project matrix. Key: A = architecture; BS = building services; Ci = civil engineering; Co = construction; S = structural engineering.

PROJECT TEAM This is appropriate in an organization which has an ongoing need for staff dedicated to managing projects (Figure 7.7). For example, a retail firm with multiple outlets may have a need for the repetitive construction of new stores.

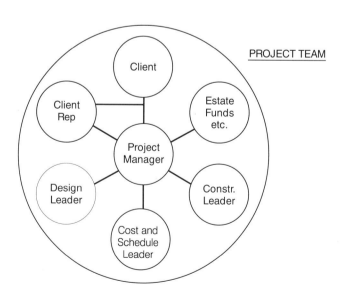

Figure 7.7 Project team structure.

MANAGEMENT STRUCTURES

Choose any two of the typical management structures described in this chapter and, using a diagram, show your understanding of how they operate.

PROJECT PLANNING AND PROGRAMMING

It is not possible to explain in detail here the techniques commonly used in project management but you should be aware of their existence.

It is widely accepted that one of the most important criteria for judging a project's success is time. As the expression goes, 'time is money' and in any project every day will have a consequential cost. If the project runs according to plan, there is less likely to be a budget overspend.

The project manager will expect to be involved from conception to completion (and in some cases in the operation of the finished product as well). This will entail:

- conceptualization of the overall process;
- planning in detail at every stage;
- integration of all the relevant information;
- execution of the work by project teams;
- continuous monitoring and evaluation;
- review and rectification if necessary.

THE MASTER PLAN OF THE PROJECT

This tool will be used to govern the overall process from beginning to end. Its preparation will be influenced by:

- the scope of the works;
- the requirements on the design team;
- the costs involved;
- the contract strategy.

From the basic information gathered initially, detailed plans can be prepared in such a way as to increase coordination of all involved. The result will be an increased chance of achieving the project objectives.

At the preliminary stage the project manager will break the process down into the major elements such as designing, planning and construction. The skill lies in ensuring that these are all integrated and support one another.

PROGRAMMING TECHNIQUES

There are various ways of carrying out planning and scheduling in a systematic way. Many of these have their origin in the United States in industries not associated with construction, e.g. the development of the Polaris missile in the 1950s. The techniques include:

- bar (or Gantt) charts;
- critical path methods;
- precedence diagramming method;
- programme evaluation and review technique (PERT);
- line of balance.

The use of computers has greatly assisted in the application of specialized packages which support these techniques. The selection of a package depends on the various factors already considered. It should allow certain essential tasks to be carried out:

- Control of resources.
- Monitoring of usage of resources.
- Progress evaluation.
- Ensuring that the client's objective will be satisfied.
- Regular decision making as and when required.

The use of the programming techniques is regarded as being essential for the day-to-day running of the construction phase. As you will increasingly become aware, once work has started on site the nature of construction means that the operations are highly interdependent. The consequence is that any delay in one will have a knock-on effect on another, which could cause late completion of the whole project. Equally important will be the increased likelihood of going over the budget allocation and thus of more money being required.

As a prerequisite to preparing programmes it will be necessary to estimate the likely durations of activities, whether they comprise a major part of the overall process (i.e. design) or an individual construction activity such as carrying out brickwork. This is simply a matter of dividing the amount of work required to be carried out by the capability of the resources available. For a definite quantity of work, estimators will be able to provide the production rate for a gang.

EXAMPLE:

Concrete required = 100 m^3.

It is estimated that a gang of 3 labourers can lay 5 m^3 of concrete per day.

100 m^3 ÷ 5 m^3 = 20 days

Assuming that the resource basis is unchanged, 20 days will be the duration inserted into the programme.

For less definite work (e.g. planning, designing, etc.) such calculations rely on the skill of the professionals involved to can give their 'best' estimates. It is then up to the project manager to decide whether this is an acceptable duration. If not, further resource allocation must be considered, with consequential cost implications, in order to meet the needs of the overall objectives of the project.

BAR CHARTS   These are also called Gantt charts after their inventor, Henry L. Gantt, who developed them during the First World War. As Figure 7.8 shows, the chart usually represents time on a horizontal scale and activities vertically. A line is drawn against each activity to represent its duration. It can then be clearly seen when the activity will start and finish.

This is the commonest form of planning technique and its popularity lies in its ease of use as a communication tool. Often it is used as a pictorial representation of what is planned, even though other more complex methods of calculation and decision making for programming may have been used already.

The bar chart has the virtue of being simple but it does have the limitation of not adequately showing the interdependence of activities.

CRITICAL PATH METHOD   This method shows the interdependence of activities because the chart is plotted like a motorway system and will normally have various routes. Some will be shorter than others, but the main interest is the longest one. This is called the critical path because the project is not fully completed until every activity is achieved. Thus the shorter routes will allow 'spare' time, which is called 'float', but the critical path determines the overall duration of the whole project (Figure 7.9).

The main advantage of this method is that it is possible to use the float of those activities not on the critical path to change resources to achieve optimal usage. It is possible to shorten the critical path but this will require more resource usage on some of the activities on the critical path. This will usually incur cost and must be judged against the need for the project to finish earlier. Care is required in carrying this out and it is possible to make a critical path shorter than one which was previously not critical but now is.

PRECEDENCE DIAGRAMMING METHOD   This works in the same way as the critical path method but with a difference in presentation: a box is normally used to present the activities. In this box are smaller boxes for the data required for calculations (Figure 7.10b). In the critical path method, the convention is for the arrows to

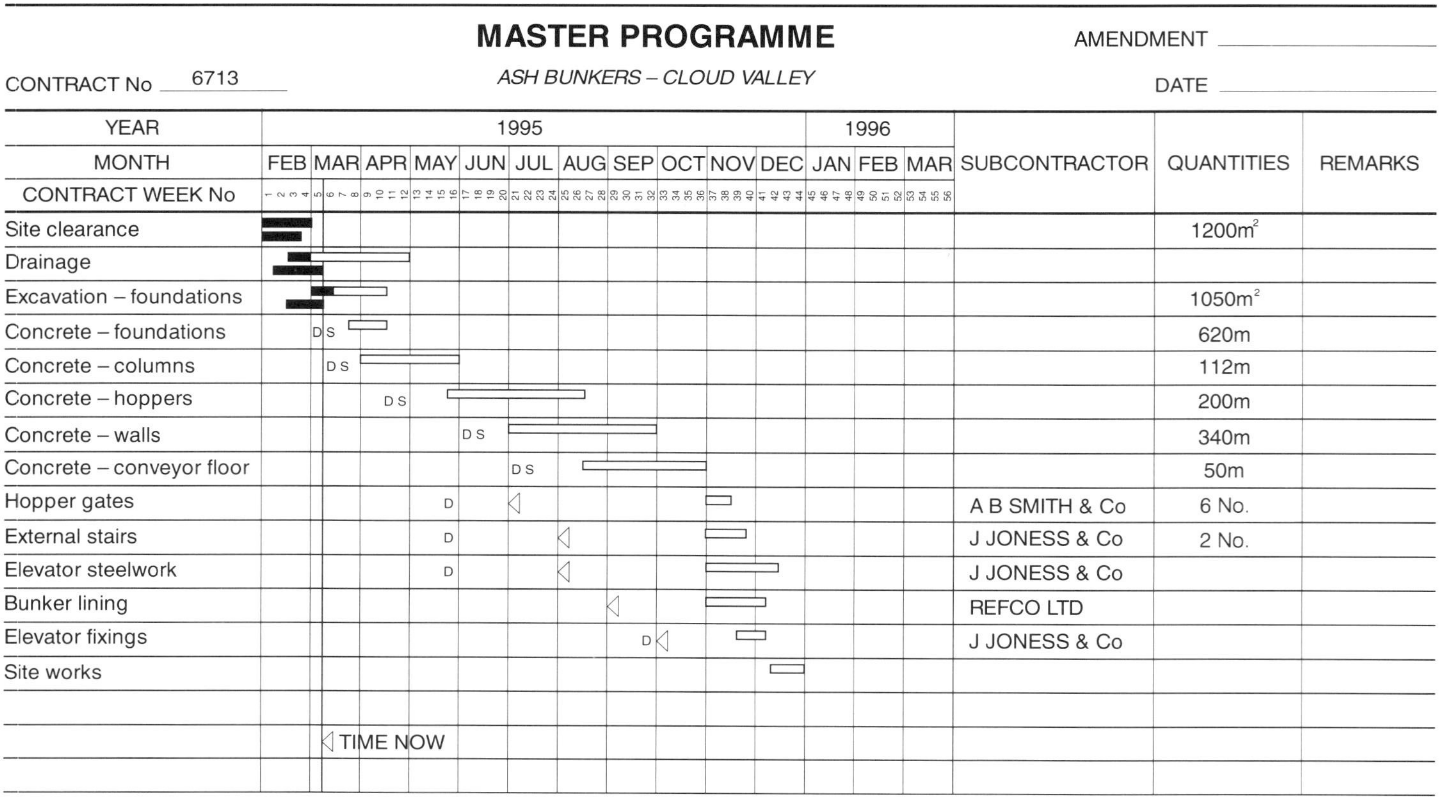

MASTER PROGRAMME

ASH BUNKERS – CLOUD VALLEY

CONTRACT No _____ 6713

AMENDMENT _____

DATE _____

CONTRACT WEEK No	1995 FEB–DEC / 1996 JAN–MAR (weeks 1–56)	SUBCONTRACTOR	QUANTITIES	REMARKS
Site clearance			1200m²	
Drainage				
Excavation – foundations			1050m²	
Concrete – foundations			620m	
Concrete – columns			112m	
Concrete – hoppers			200m	
Concrete – walls			340m	
Concrete – conveyor floor			50m	
Hopper gates		A B SMITH & Co	6 No.	
External stairs		J JONESS & Co	2 No.	
Elevator steelwork		J JONESS & Co		
Bunker lining		REFCO LTD		
Elevator fixings		J JONESS & Co		
Site works				

Key: D = drawings; S = bar schedule; ▽ = place order.

TIME NOW

Figure 7.8 Typical bar chart. Key: D = drawings; S = bar schedule; ▽ = place order. (Source: Pilcher, R. (1992) *Principles of Construction Management*, McGraw Hill, p. 265.)

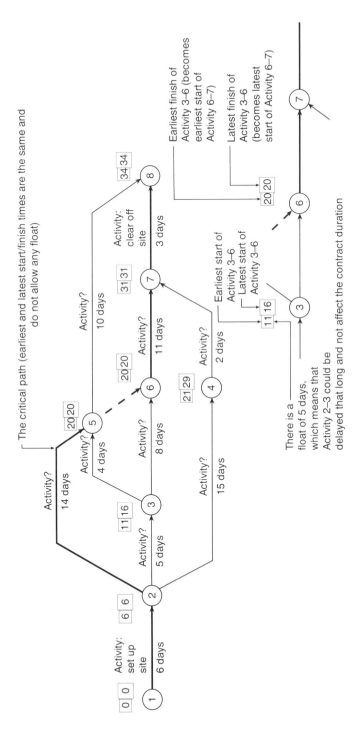

Figure 7.9 Typical critical path method (network).

Notes:

1. Length of arrows not drawn to suit durations.
2. Number the nodes (circles).
3. Boxes for earliest and latest start and finish times.
4. Activities identified by event numbers, i.e. 2–3 or 5–8, etc., to prevent misunderstandings during discussions or over the telephone.

(Source: Forster, G. (1986) *Building Organisation and Procedures*, Longman, p. 264.)

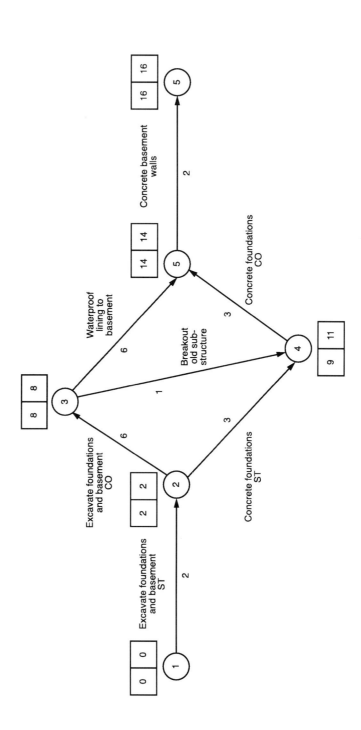

Figure 7.10 (a) Typical critical path: a network showing durations, event numbers and event times. (Source: Harris, F. and McCaffer, R. (1983) *Modern Construction Management*, p. 15.)

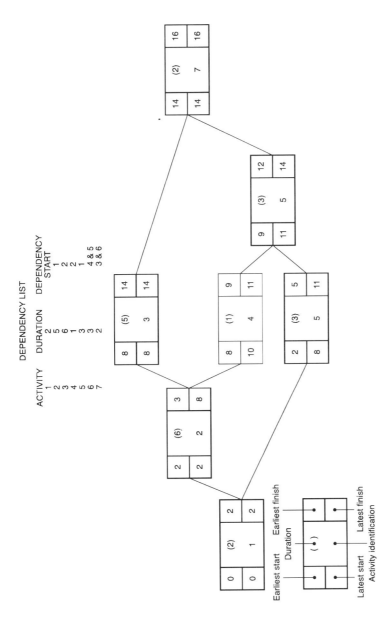

Figure 7.10 (b) Precedence list and precedence diagram showing the same network as in (a). (Source: Harris, F. and McCaffer, R. (1983) *Modern Construction Management*, p. 22.)

represent the activity and the circles ('nodes') to be 'milestones' at the beginning of an activity, or at the end of the preceding one. In the precedence method, the connecting lines between the boxes represent the logic of the sequence.

Which method you use is really a matter of choice – the result of calculations will be the same for both. The essential task is to work out those activities with float and those without float. The latter will be those whose timing will be crucial and which must start and finish at the programme time. Failure to do so will cause delay to the overall programme, and thus additional cost.

PERT   The Programme Evaluation and Review Technique of planning and programming was developed by the US Navy for the production of Polaris missiles. Its use is based on statistical principles and gives the programmer the most probable project duration based on information available. At the same time it can also give the most pessimistic duration (i.e. the longest time to complete) and the most optimistic. With the use of computers, it is possible to change the input information and thus alter the duration of a project to suit. Given good initial information of the likely time to complete pieces of work, this is an excellent method of scientific planning (Figure 7.11).

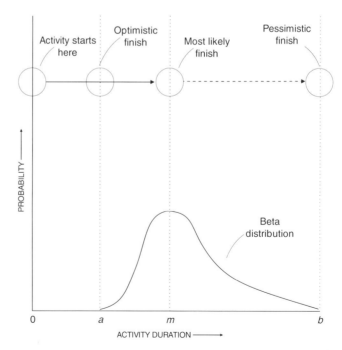

Figure 7.11 PERT diagram. (Source: Pilcher, R. (1976) *Principles of Construction Management*, McGraw Hill, p. 180.)

LINE OF BALANCE   This programming method is most appropriate where the work being carried out is repetitive. The guiding principle is that there is a need to maintain a given schedule. A good example would be for a number of housing units to be completed each week.

The method involves working out the rate of production for each of the sub-elements (Trades) which make up the complete unit. This allows a line to be drawn on the diagram which shows the rate that can be achieved with given resources. By changing the resource input, you can alter the slope of the line and consequently the rate of production. It is important that the lines do not cross because the logical sequence would then be destroyed. For example, you cannot put the roof on a building before you have constructed the walls or structures to support it.

The main use of this system is in attempting to follow the example of factory-type production, and thus make the process continuous. If the rate of production is not regular, the actual rate will deviate from that shown on the diagram and thus rectification (using more resources) will be required (Figure 7.12).

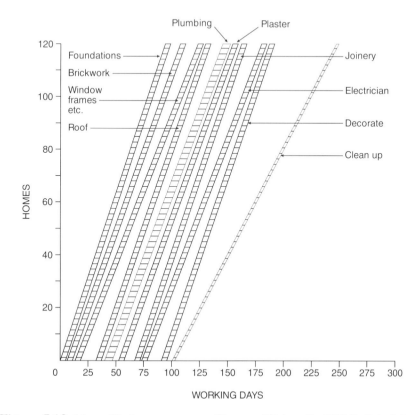

Figure 7.12 Line of balance diagram. (Source: Pilcher, R. (1992) *Principles of Construction Management*, McGraw Hill, p. 363.)

WORKPIECE 7.5

PLANNING METHODS

Why is an accurate planning system essential to the successful management of a project?

Briefly show your understanding of the appropriateness of the following types of planning method for particular situations:

- Bar chart.
- Critical path.
- Line of balance.

SUMMARY

The purpose of this chapter has been to explore the basic features of project management in construction. This will give an understanding of the role that can be played by this discipline and why it is needed. It has also shown how all professionals play their part in forming their relationships in developing a 'project team'.

The importance of the skills required for a good project manager have been demonstrated. You should be aware of what they are and how you can attempt to develop them during your period of study.

CHECKLIST

The issues covered in this chapter are:

- the emergence of the role of project management;
- why this role has become so influential;
- the need for a new emphasis and change in traditional methods of operation;
- definition of project management;
- the importance of teamwork and communication;
- the use of alternative structures and organization;
- methods of project planning and programming.

REFERENCES

1. Ball, M. (1988) *Rebuilding Construction – Economic Change in the British Construction Industry*, Routledge.
2. Hilton, W. (1968) *Industrial Relations in Construction*, Pergamon Press.
3. Higgin, G. and Jessop, N. (1965) *Communications in the Building Industry: the report of a Pilot Study*, Tavistock Institute.
4. Hillebrandt, P.M., Andrew, J., Bale, J. and Smith, T. (1974) *Project Management: Proposals for Change*, Building Economics Research Unit, University College Environmental Research Group.
5. Walker, A. (1984) *Project Management in Construction*, BSP Professional.
6. Chevin, D. (1993) Project management: variety performers. *Building*, 6 August.

7.   *Concise English Dictionary* (1986), Harper Collins.
8.   Hamilton, B. (1990) Project management: key characteristics. *New Builder*, 21 June.

FURTHER READING

Callahan, M.T, Quackenbush, D.G and Rowings, E. (1992) *Construction Project Scheduling*, McGraw Hill.

Pilcher, R. (1992) *Principles of Construction Management*, McGraw Hill.

Reiss, G. (1992) *Project Management Demystified (Today's Tools and Techniques)*, E & FN Spon.

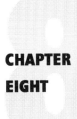

THE DEVELOPMENT INDUSTRY AND COMMUNITY INITIATIVES

TOM MUIR,
WITH CONTRIBUTIONS FROM
JOHN DAVISON, MAURICE INGRAM,
RICHARD TURKINGTON AND
PATRICK LOFTMAN

THEME

The theme of this chapter is partnership – not between professional groups in the development team, as in Chapter 3, but partnership which incorporates community groups within society. It discusses different case studies of community initiatives in the development industry which demonstrate different models of such partnerships. The case studies also demonstrate management structures for bridging professional 'mystique' and demystifying the nature of professional services in the development industry.

OBJECTIVES

After reading this chapter you should be able to:

- understand the nature of community-based initiatives in the development industry;

- compare the purposes of, and partnership arrangements in, each case study.

In most of the preceding chapters the cooperation and collaboration described has been between members of the building team or partners within the development industry. In this chapter we will focus on links between the industry and the communities for whom the development is intended.

Some early seeds of this collaboration can be seen in the nineteenth century with Robert Owen's New Lanark and later on Ebenezer Howard's cooperatively managed garden cities. However, it was not really until legislation on town planning in the 1940s and subsequent reports such as the Skeffington Report[1] that a real growth in community involvement partnership developed.

Programmes in various forms have developed as a series of quite separate ventures in the last 15–20 years. Recently the government has identified partnership arrangements as a prerequisite for attracting public funding. Each partnership arrangement is established to address a different problem, but they share the prime basic objective of attempting to pull together both the providers and the users of the development industry and its products. Their introduction has been the result of action by many different members of the team. Some are set up by central and local government as a means of channelling resources into a particular area identified as being in need; others are the product of professional concern regarding the effectiveness of links with clients' needs.

It is useful at this point to refer to Chapter 5, where the nature of partnership in the development process is considered. That chapter also provides a helpful guide to the introduction of such programmes in terms of land use and property management. In particular it describes the increasing role that the private sector has begun to play in partnership projects. City Challenge, for example, is described in the following series of case studies and is also included in Chapter 5 as a case where resources were created through the action of a city council, attracting government grants, and employing a variety of built environment professional skills linked with community action.

THE DEVELOPMENT OF COMMUNITY INITIATIVES IN PARTNERSHIP SCHEMES

Since about 1980 there has been an increase in non-profitmaking agencies, promoted by central government to provide a new approach to the solution of intractable urban problems. As Chapter 4 suggests, these single-service agencies may be neither public nor private (in the accepted sense) but represent a new form of partnership. Government funding is invariably based upon establishing an effective partnership between public bodies and community and business interests.

The following case studies are examples of this type of partnership arrangement. They stress the extent of community involvement in the development process and describe different kinds of approach.

The first example, that of the Groundwork Trust, typifies how government has supported this kind of approach and provided for partnership arrangements in the field of urban regeneration.

The second and third examples describe community initiatives that have been promoted and supported by professional bodies, namely the Royal Institute of British Architects and the Royal Town Planning Institute, and have also attracted government support.

The fourth example, Housing Action Trusts, is clearly linked with government legislation on privatization as described in Chapter 4, but again adopts similar partnership arrangements.

The fifth and final example, City Challenge, returns to the theme of urban regeneration as an area of project approach by central government but relying on local ideas and partnerships for its success.

There are many more examples of community initiatives in partnership schemes which you may be aware of and which you may wish to compare with the examples given.

THE GROUNDWORK TRUST

John Davison

The Groundwork Trust's mission is: 'Environmental regeneration in partnership with the community, voluntary and environmental organizations, public authorities and business in order to achieve quality, sustainable improvements to the environment.'

Its approach to environmental regeneration recognizes the complexity of our present cities. Sustainable improvements require contributions from all sectors and Groundwork has been developed to make it possible for public bodies, commercial companies, voluntary organizations and individuals in society to work together to achieve practical and worthwhile results.

Since the launch of Operation Groundwork in 1981, Groundwork has developed and grown to more than 30 trusts. Each trust is established with a clear objective to bring about local environmental regeneration through a partnership with the local community. Local ownership is an essential facet of the approach and individual trusts develop their own programmes based on local needs.

PARTNERSHIP AGREEMENTS

Each trust is founded by a partnership of local authorities, business and voluntary organizations and the Groundwork Foundation, which is the national coordinating body for the network. The founding partners enter into a partnership agreement to secure core funding for the new trust during its initial six years of operation.

Once established, each trust derives its own policies and programmes based on an assessment of local needs and involving local partners. Thus, day-to-day programmes of trusts vary from location to location within the overall framework laid down by the Groundwork network.

Trusts operate under the following principles when undertaking their programmes.

ENVIRONMENTAL REGENERATION Groundwork was established in response to the clear need for environmental improvement on the fringes of our towns and cities. While this continues to form a major priority for many Groundwork trusts, the Groundwork approach has proved to be effective in urban and some rural areas.

COMMUNITY Groundwork's approach is founded on the need to involve and empower local communities in caring for their local environment. It does this by assisting local groups and organizations to realize their objectives where these objectives are within the remit of the Groundwork Trust. It is committed to the principles and practice of equal opportunity and identifies each sector within the local community to provide opportunities for local people to become involved in the development and implementation of Trust projects and programmes.

EDUCATION Each trust has a central objective to increase awareness and educate about the environment. Each trust seeks to raise awareness of environmental issues throughout the community, develops and promotes a set of 'key' messages and seeks to develop concern for global issues. Local action is based on the theme of 'think global and act local'.

SECURING RESOURCES Support during the establishment of each Groundwork initiative is provided through the Groundwork Foundation and local sponsors. However, it is the overall responsibility of each trust to secure the resources to sustain the trust and undertake a programme of activity.

Each Groundwork trust is separately constituted and responsible for its own programmes and activities within its operational area. One of Groundwork's strengths, however, is that each local trust is a member of a national network.

TRUST ROLES

Groundwork is a flexible mechanism for environmental regeneration and trusts are likely to fulfil a range of roles on projects. For example, a trust may:

- act as initiator of projects;
- respond to the initiative of others;
- act as a facilitator or enabler, assisting others to undertake schemes;
- manage projects directly;
- act as client or agent;
- act as contractor;
- be based on an assessment of local needs;
- involve the local community;
- include partnerships with others;
- be involved in a variety of roles;
- balance the need to fulfil the trust's objectives with the need to generate income.

COMMUNITY ARCHITECTURE

Tom Muir

The Community Architecture movement was born out of the public's disenchantment with the results of the post-war building boom and its products. Housing, in particular, was seen to be a product more of social engineering and design dogma than a response to people's needs.

The combination of two factors – massive housing programmes initiated by local authorities under pressure from central government, and sophisticated prefabricated site assembly building systems which were only cost effective in massive-scale projects – led to a credibility gap developing between suppliers and consumers.

Community Architecture was a response to this situation and soon built up a following amongst practising architects who recognized the dangers to both the industry and the profession being posed by this gap.[2] In general, the motivation of this movement has been the demystification of the architectural service so as to enable meaningful contact to be made between designer and user. Community architects claim that traditional practice reinforces the mystique and denies the architect essential exposure to ideas and information which can only be provided by the user.

Community architecture evolved out of a series of initiatives, examples of which included the following.

BYKER REDEVELOPMENT (RALPH ERSKINE, 1970)

The redevelopment of this area of Newcastle-upon-Tyne was carried out in a manner which gave most of the existing residents an opportunity to contribute to the architect's brief. The architect, Ralph Erskine and Partners, set up an office in the centre of the area of old nineteenth century houses which were to be developed. The residents were even consulted as to whether they wanted their area to be rehabilitated, retaining the existing houses and streets, or redeveloped. They chose the latter.

The local office was manned by a partner and the design team. Local residents were encouraged to 'drop in' and discuss how they saw the future development of their housing. The decision had already been taken that only people who wished to be moved out of the area would go; the rest would be rehoused in the new development.

This experiment in making such a direct link between the designer and user proved most successful and contributed to the residents feeling that they were part of the process and not simply faceless occupants. Subsequent evaluation of the project has supported this conclusion. However, its real success was achieved because little compromise was made to good modern, innovative design principles, and because its solution to the incorporation of an acoustic barrier to protect the residents from a proposed motorway produced a design which is held in high esteem by architects throughout the world.

MACCLESFIELD HOUSING ASSOCIATION (ROD HACKNEY ASSOCIATES)

In the late 1970s, housing associations gradually began to replace local authorities as the main providers of housing in the rental sector. This resulted in smaller developments with more intimate relationships between the association committee, the professionals and – where they were known – the residents. Rod Hackney, an architect in practice in Macclesfield, established through a housing association a close working partnership with a group of residents and together they worked on a programme of rehabilitation and rebuilding for their area.

This scheme is of seminal importance in the Community Architecture movement. Its organizational structure whereby all the participants – architect, quantity surveyor, engineer, planner and builder – worked closely with the association committee and the residents became a model for many subsequent projects.

ARCHITECTURE 'SHOPS'

Some architects in the late 1970s recognized that the very format of an architect's professional office was not friendly to the general public, who were the ultimate users of their 'product' and, as such, the final arbiters of their success or failure. The idea of the shop evolved as being a more familiar point of contact when a service was required and many architects moved their offices, previously located in areas surrounded by other offices, to shopping locations. This more familiar environment, with the offices often sited in a row of shops, helped to break down the mystique that so often surrounds professional activities and the subsequent suspicion and mistrust it engenders.

THE COMMUNITY ARCHITECTURE GROUP

As a result of the experience of projects such as the ones we have discussed, the Royal Institute of British Architects created the Community Architecture Group to develop and support schemes like these throughout the country.[3] The group was first formed in the early 1970s and has attracted extensive national and international interest. It was one of the few aspects of architecture that HRH Prince Charles enthusiastically supported at the time of his criticism of modern architecture as a whole, and it has had a considerable effect on the way architects and others have contributed to urban regeneration.

PLANNING AID

Maurice Ingram

Planning Aid is the provision of free and independent professional advice about town planning to groups and individuals who cannot afford to pay consultants' fees. The service is offered by volunteer planners who deal with similar problems in the course of their work and therefore have wide knowledge of the planning system.

Planning Aid is not part of central or local government but is an independent charity, largely funded by the Royal Town Planning Institute, which is the professional body responsible for ensuring that the standards and training of town planners are maintained.[4]

The key objective of Planning Aid is to enable community groups and individuals to gain access to and play a part in the planning system. It enables them to assess their immediate or long-term problems or choices, to prepare their own plans and to articulate their response to the plans of others.

The type of help given by Planning Aid includes:

- whom to contact in local authorities about a planning problem;
- information on planning procedures;
- help with understanding the many types of plans prepared by district and county councils;
- applying for planning permission;
- appealing against the refusal of planning permission;
- making individuals or local community voices heard when plans are being drawn up;

● appearing at public inquiries.

Planning Aid makes a particular effort to reach individuals and groups previously excluded from the planning system. A good example of this emphasis is the work of the West Midlands Planning Aid Service. In 1992 they secured funding from Birmingham City Council's inner city partnership programme for a 5-month pilot project to promote and develop the service among disadvantaged groups in the inner city area. Over 20 existing community groups and organizations were involved in promoting their work, publicity work was carried out with the local media, local schools were involved and leaflets produced in six ethnic minority languages. In a 4-month period the project generated more than 60 cases, ranging from advice on planning applications to objections to development proposals and the formulating of community planning initiatives. The highest proportion of groups and individuals helped was Asian, followed by Afro-Caribbean, White and Chinese.

The project emphasized the need for planning aid in the inner city, and the West Midlands Planning Aid Service now employs an inner-city worker as a direct result of the project. The service is also now much more proactive in undertaking outreach work among local communities. In addition the project has encouraged the city council to give greater priority to involving the local communities in town planning and it now works closely with the Planning Aid Service to achieve this objective.

To quote Silvera, the inner-city worker of West Midlands Planning Aid Service:[5] 'While Planning Aid may be unable to alleviate many of our clients' day-to-day problems, it does enable many people, particularly those excluded from the planning arena, to have some say about decisions which affect their lives.'

HOUSING ACTION TRUSTS

Richard Turkington

The origins of Housing Action Trusts were firmly located in central government efforts, during the 1980s, to wrest control of council housing from local housing authorities. Of the measures introduced during this decade, none has gone through such a transformation. Consequently, the trusts which exist in the 1990s look very different from those planned in the 1980s, a tribute to concerted tenant action and local political initiative.

Housing Action Trusts (HATs) have their origins in the 1987 Conservative Party manifesto which envisaged the creation of 'corporations' to take over the management and refurbishment of large, run-down local authority estates as a prelude to a transfer of ownership.[6]

HAT estates were to be selected by the Department of the Environment and, whilst tenants were to be consulted, they had no right of veto. Decision making and financial gains made from the sale of land and renovated properties were to be used to provide financial support for the programme. A White Paper was issued in September 1987 and legislation was passed in the following year to enable the scheme to be launched (Housing Act, 1988, Part III).

Eighteen estates in the local authority areas of Lambeth, Leeds, Sandwell, Southwark, Sunderland and Tower Hamlets were initially selected. However, none came to fruition and ultimately a different set of estates is now being managed as 'Housing Action Trusts'. Karn[7] had identified four phases in the evolution of the HAT concept.

In the 'legislative' phase (from September 1987 to November 1988), powerful and unexpected tenant opposition began to develop. The government first conceded the option of estates returning to local authority control and then tenant ballots on participation in the scheme.

In the second 'feasibility study' phase (from July 1988) consultants began to investigate local conditions in the six pilot areas. The major findings were: that the cost of refurbishment would be much higher than anticipated; that estate problems were not limited to the physical fabric; and that tenant suspicion and hostility were very high. A rethinking of the scheme led to a focus on nine estates in five areas, with the London Borough of Tower Hamlets now excluded.[8]

The third 'ballots' phase began in March 1989, and despite government attempts to reaffirm the option of a return to local authority control, tenant opposition was overwhelming. Only two 'official' ballots were ever undertaken (on the North Peckham and Gloucester Grove Estates in Southwark) and they produced 'no' votes of 67% and 73% respectively. A combination of unofficial ballots, questioning consultants' reports and local authority opposition undermined the HAT programme, which by now had cost over £3 million.

Ironically, the local authority sector, which had been so alienated by the scheme, now offered an alternative. In November 1989, the 'local authority' phase began with consideration by the London Borough of Waltham Forest of the relevance of the HAT concept for refurbishing four of its panel-construction estates. Tenant consultation was already under way and, consequently, local people were in a position to negotiate on their own behalf. The outcome was that, with strong tenant representation on the management board, 81% of tenants voted in favour, and work began in April 1991.[9] In the meantime, Hull City Council had begun its own private negotiations to establish a North Hull HAT involving 2000 interwar houses. A similarly locally controlled process achieved a 69% 'yes' vote in March 1991, although with the lead taken by the local authority.

Whilst the original legislation had been used, these two pioneering HATs changed the original approach in two important respects: firstly, the Waltham Forest HAT had been strongly tenant-led, in contrast to the effective 'disenfranchisment' of tenants in the early proposals and secondly, the North Hull HAT had been strongly led by the local authority, in contrast to the initial exclusion of this sector.

The willingness of central government to accept such initiatives, in order to keep the HAT concept alive, has encouraged a final 'emulation' phase in the HAT saga with schemes in Birmingham (Castle Vale), Liverpool, Stonebridge/Brent and Tower Hamlets. The most surprising of these, and marking a shift away from an estate-based notion of refurbishment, is the Liverpool HAT which includes all the city's 71 tower blocks containing 5337 flats on 35 sites. The local authority began negotiations in April 1991 and, following a favourable tenant ballot, the HAT was established in February 1993. The final HAT to be established was at Castle Vale, Birmingham, and once again problems of inadequate resources to refurbish a mainly tower block estate encouraged the local authority to explore the HAT alternative. A ballot held in March 1993 approved the creation of the HAT and work is now under way on improvements costing £130 million.

Housing Action Trusts now have responsibility for over 18 000 homes and are providing a useful testing ground for locally targeted and comprehensive estate improvement in which tenants have a significant input. This is achieved through tenant representation on the management board (typically four of the 11 members) and through extensive consultation on changes to dwellings and estates. Ironically, a centrally determined scheme which was planned without consulting tenants is providing a model of what can be achieved when local authorities and tenants are able to lead the way.

City Challenge was launched by Michael Heseltine (then Secretary of State for the Environment) in May 1991 as a new and radical approach to the regeneration of declining urban areas. Under the City Challenge initiative local authorities were given the lead role in devising imaginative

CITY CHALLENGE

Patrick Loftman

regeneration strategies for deprived areas within their boundaries. In developing a vision statement and action plans for their areas, however, the local authorities were required to do so in partnership with other local 'actors', in particular local businesses, community groups and other public agencies such as police and health authorities.

Under City Challenge two 'competitions' were held whereby local authorities were invited to form partnerships with public, private and community sector interests to tackle the physical, social and economic problems in chosen disadvantaged areas. In the first 'pilot' competition, held in 1991, 17 urban local authorities were invited to bid for £37.5 million each, over a 5-year period. Each local authority was given only 6 weeks by central government to bring together its potential partners, select a target area, consult local people, formulate 'vision statements' and draw together detailed 5-year plans.

The successful bids were then developed further into firm action plans – detailing firm commitments to action and how they would be delivered. In the second competition, launched in February 1992, all 57 local authorities defined as urban priority areas were invited to bid for City Challenge with 20 winners announced in July 1992.

HOW CITY CHALLENGE DIFFERED FROM OTHER DOE INITIATIVES
According to central government, City Challenge was different from previous Department of the Environment urban regeneration initiatives in three ways:

1. It sought to concentrate resources (both public and private) within a clearly defined geographical area, whereas previously resources were deemed to have been spread too thinly over too wide an area.

2. Previous government inner city programmes had focused on giving help to individual organizations or sectors directly, without encouraging cooperation between them. City Challenge, on the other hand, aimed to bring organizations within a locality to work together in partnership to secure sustainable urban regeneration.

3. City Challenge introduced a system of competitive bidding for central government resources, in contrast to a more mechanical process, and the government argues that this has led to more imaginative and innovative approaches to addressing inner city problems.[10]

After securing government approval and funding, City Challenge partnerships formed Boards to manage the regeneration process and ensure that objectives set out in their 5-year Action Plan are achieved. Members of the City Challenge Board usually include local authority representatives, local business people such as developers, employers and firms, residents, tenants and community organizations and representatives from other public agencies such as the police and health services. Each of the partners brings different skills, expertise and knowledge to the task of regenerating disadvantaged areas. Local authorities, given their wide service delivery and planning responsibilities, are in an ideal position to lead the regeneration process and bring together the various partners, whilst the private sector is able to contribute considerable resources and experience to bring about physical change and generate wealth and employment opportunities. Local communities, on the other hand, bring with them considerable experience and knowledge about local needs and issues and are in the best position to ensure that current local people benefit from the regeneration process.

The precise profile of partners involved in City Challenge partnerships varies according to the different local circumstances in each area. In the Newtown South Aston City Challenge initiative in Birmingham, for example, there are 15 directors – four elected from the local community, four from the local authority, three from the private sector, and three from other public sector agencies (the principal of a local further education college, the deputy chief probation officer and a senior West Midlands Health Authority officer). The Board in each City Challenge area is supported by an implementation team of officers led by a chief executive.

WORKPIECE 8.1

PROFESSIONAL/COMMUNITY PARTNERSHIPS

Take one of the five examples of professional/community partnership projects and try to describe the roles of the various built environment professionals in the team.

Indicate how these roles might differ from those found in more traditional projects.

WORKPIECE 8.2

ANALYSIS OF PARTNERSHIP SCHEMES

A common thread running through all of the examples is the increasing incorporation of the user into the professional process. There is also the recognition that the provider is not necessarily the user. A diagram reflecting this might be as shown here:

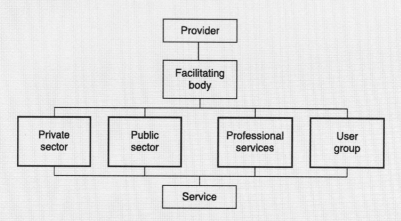

Partnership analysis: providers and users.

Using this diagram as a basis, draw similar diagrams of each of the examples in this chapter.

WORKPIECE 8.3

PROFESSIONAL BODY INSTITUTE INVOLVEMENT IN PARTNERSHIP SCHEMES

Select the professional body with which you are most familiar and indicate different ways in which it could develop partnership ventures such as those referred to in this chapter.

If your profession is primarily in the private sector, suggest how commercial viability could be achieved. If it is primarily in the public sector, indicate how implementation is achieved to the satisfaction of both the resource providers and the users.

WORKPIECE 8.4

A CASE STUDY OF ENGLISH HERITAGE

Investigate the partnership arrangements of English Heritage and compare these arrangements with the case studies included in this chapter.

SUMMARY

These five examples all share at least one common objective and that is the involvement of residents in development projects. The teams vary considerably in their composition, from the possibility of only one professional being involved (in the example of Community Architecture) to a partnership between central government, local government, local businesses and community associations as is the case with Housing Action Trusts (HATs). Community Architecture and Planning Aid are clearly attempts to penetrate a process which is often seen as substantially 'top down' and bureaucratic, to ensure that everyone has the opportunity to benefit from it and not feel excluded.

Groundwork Trust is an example of a community-based initiative that has attracted central government funding, in contrast to Housing Action Trusts which are primarily driven by central government, but cannot operate without effective partnership with local residents. The two abortive attempts to develop HATs without such cooperation demonstrate this. The City Challenge scheme, which also attracts government funding, is a partnership between local government, local businesses and the community in inner city areas.

These examples present built environment professionals with a new and more complex series of roles. It is necessary to identify to what extent the brief is a composite 'programme' from all partners in the project; therefore, once more, the professional must become a member of a team in which his professional skills and advice form a part of a collective decision-making process. In such projects, the traditional concept of a client is blurred as the team works together towards a collectively defined objective. Initiatives like those considered above have provided further challenges to the conventional roles of the built environment professions.

CHECKLIST

The issues covered in this chapter are the challenges presented to the built environment professions by community initiatives, such as:

- Groundwork Trust;
- Community Architecture;
- Planning Aid;
- Housing Action Trusts;
- City Challenge.

REFERENCES

1. HMSO (1969) *People and Plans, The Skeffington Report*, HMSO, London.
2. Wates, N. and Knevitt, C. (1987) *Community Architecture: How people are creating their own environments*, Penguin.

3.   RIBA (1978) *The Practice of Community Architecture: The Case for a Community Aid Fund*, Royal Institute of British Architects, London.

4.   RTPI (1992) *The Management and Operation of RTPI Planning Aid Services*, Royal Town Planners Institute, London.

5.   Silvera, I. (1993) Birmingham Pilot for Inner City Planning Aid. *Planning*, **1039**, 8 October.

6.   Dennis, F. (1990) HATs – Who Needs Them? *Housing*, Nov., pp 14–15.

7.   Karn, V. (1993) Remodelling a HAT: the implementation of the Housing Action Trust legislation 1987–92, in *Implementing Housing Policy* (eds P. Malpass and R. Means), Open University Press.

8.   Woodward, R. (1991) Mobilising opposition: the campaign against Housing Action Trusts in Tower Hamlets. *Housing Studies*, Vol. 6, no. 1, January, pp. 44–56.

9.   Ridout, G. (1994) Tenants' lather, the Waltham Forest HAT. *Building*, 28 January, pp. 50–54.

10. DOE (1994) *City Challenge: Partnerships Regenerating England's Urban Areas*, Department of the Environment, London.

FURTHER READING

Atkinson, R. and Moon, G. (1994) *Urban Policy in Britain: the City, the State and the Market*, Macmillan.

MacFarlane, R. (1993) *Community Involvement in City Challenge: A policy report*, National Council for Voluntary Organisations, London.

MacFarlane, R. and Mabbot, J. (1993) *City Challenge: Involving local communities*, National Council for Voluntary Organisations.

Newman, O. (1972) *Defensible Space*, Macmillan.

New Architecture Movement (Public Design Group) (1978) *Community Architecture; A Public Design Service*, report to the Ministry of Housing and Construction, London.

Scott, J. and Jenks, M. (1986) *What is the point of Community Architecture?*, Working Paper No. 95, Department of Town Planning, Oxford Polytechnic, Oxford.

Sneddon, J. and Theobald, C. (eds) (1987) *Building Communities: The First International Conference on Community Architecture*, Planning and Design, London.

Woolley, T. (ed.) (1985) *The Characteristics of Community Architecture and Community Technical Aid*, occasional paper, Department of Architecture and Building Science, University of Strathclyde.

Woolley, T. (1985) *Community Architecture: an Evaluation of the Case for User Participation in Architectural Design*, Department of Architecture, Oxford Polytechnic.

THE DEVELOPMENT INDUSTRY AND SUSTAINABILITY

RICHARD COLES

THEME

What does the word 'sustainable' mean? Why is it so important? What implications will sustainability have for the built environment professionals? As one of many species living on the earth, we are still seeking to find the most appropriate relationship with the environment.

In this chapter we examine ideas about how to develop such a relationship which can fulfil our present but more importantly our future needs. Using the concept of development, this chapter explores the ideas of environmentalism and establishes a philosophy for analysing your professional development.

OBJECTIVES

After reading this chapter you should be able to:

● understand the way that humans interact with the environment;

● understand that our past and present actions have caused serious environmental degradation, and the need for change;

● understand the ideas of developing a sustainable relationship with the environment;

● explore current ideas of environmentalism within the context of your own profession.

INTRODUCTION

Environmentalism now pervades our every action as concerns over global pollution, dwindling resources and loss of species diversity characterize the final decade of the twentieth century. Our relationship with the environment is crude. The industrialization of society has left us with a legacy of environmental problems that need addressing and has led to the development of environmental philosophy. At the heart of this philosophy is the concept of sustainable development. In this chapter we shall examine the nature of development in relation to the concept of sustainability. From this we shall derive a context, or a framework in which the built environment professions can work to meet increasingly complex environmental demands. In doing so, we shall attempt to address two questions:

- What does sustainability mean?
- How does sustainability affect professional attitudes and working relationships between professions?

Do not be put off by the words 'environment' and 'environmentalist'. The **environment** is simply the place where we and our fellow creatures live. An **environmentalist** is someone who is concerned about the environment and wishes to develop a careful relationship with it and ensure that damage and degradation do not occur. Humans have always had a complex relationship with the environment[1] and current ideas of environmentalism are promoted by concern and fears about wholescale global pollution, loss of species diversity and dwindling resources.

In discussing these ideas several theoretical models involving basic ecological principles are presented. **Ecology** means a study of the home or habitat. It is concerned with relationships between organisms and their home environment and it is an appropriate discipline through which to explain ideas of sustainability.

WHAT IS A SUSTAINABLE APPROACH?

A **sustainable approach** (or sustainability) is one that can be maintained without material change, in theory indefinitely and certainly over long periods. The term **sustainability** gained common usage following the Brundtland Report.[2] It was used to express a desirable relationship with the environment whereby our present use of environmental resources would not jeopardize the abilities of future generations to use those same resources. A **sustainable relationship** means trying to maintain an environment that broadly retains its value and to ensure that that value can be passed on to our descendants.

Truly sustainable systems in nature are those where the interaction with the environment is complex but stable, i.e. an organism lives in harmony with the environment and simply perpetuates itself as a species, the whole forming an **ecosystem** – such as tropical rain forest. These systems are much studied by **ecologists**, who are concerned about the relationships between species in the ecosystem and the individual species themselves.[3] These systems are dynamic. They do not stay still. They vary, but over time they remain stable. These are systems which, by definition, are formed within the constraints of nature, particularly within the limitations of the natural supply of energy from the sun. In contrast, human populations change the nature of the environment through the exploitation of a wide range of resources, especially energy sources,[4,5] and, rather than living within the constraints of the natural environment, they have modified it extensively and purposely to meet desired requirements.

This is self-evident when we examine where we live. Urban areas clearly consist of a highly complex interaction of humans and the environment, but the same is so for other areas. In the UK and Europe the whole of the environment is highly manipulated: the apparently natural country-side is a product of intensive agriculture (Figure 9.1); most woodlands

HUMAN INTERACTION WITH THE ENVIRONMENT

Figure 9.1 Lowland farmland – natural countryside? Although apparently 'natural', this is an outstandingly diverse landscape 'manufactured' for the purpose of nineteenth century farming, emphasizing that we are able to design environments to meet our own requirements.

are a result of planned timber production; and truly natural areas are limited to a few locations on the coast and the mountain tops.

These manipulated systems can be described as 'built'. In order to 'build' them, a wide variety of professions, each with an individual philosophy, interact. Thus the environment can be described as the **built environment** in contrast to areas such as the tropical rainforests which can clearly be described as natural environment.

As humans we change the environment, and the industry that changes the environment can be defined as the **development industry**. This industry consists of a whole range of activities, which are evident in everyday life, including agriculture, road building, house construction and so on, each of which has its own complex interaction with the environment. The key point is that the development industry, as required by our social and political culture, has changed and continues to change the nature of the environment through the exploitation of resources. Until recently there has been a tendency to consider the environment as an infinite abstract resource and to divorce ourselves from nature's processes. However, this attitude cannot continue since ultimately we all live within the same global constraints. It is change brought about by human activity (human development) which has degraded the natural environment and further degradation is unacceptable. It would be fair to say that we have suddenly woken up to the environmental realities of our world.

Urgent changes in attitude are required. Literally everything we do has an environmental impact and that impact has to be identified as good, bad or benign.

ENVIRONMENTAL EQUITY

In a sustainable relationship, we must optimize environmental value and ensure that this can be passed on to future generations. However, we can modify this approach slightly by introducing the term **environmental equity** – equity in preference to value, since we are dealing with the interaction between human beings and the environment where basic environmental values are crucial but where social conditions and technical innovation are real parts of the process.[6]

The current development industry causes environmental degradation and is clearly not sustainable. Sustainable development requires a reappraisal of the development process to optimize environmental value and ensure that this can be passed on to future generations.

Figure 9.2 shows a natural system which makes use of the environment via the energy of the sun. Natural limiting factors such as the lack of food or the polluting effects of excessive waste stop the system overrunning and maintain it as stable. These factors cause negative feedback and interact on the population, keeping it in check. While individuals may not survive, the population as a whole does; hence successive generations utilize those same environmental resources. In particular note that the system uses only sunlight as the energy source, and that the waste is recycled; for example, dead plants and animals are broken down by fungi and bacteria to be reabsorbed by growing plants. The ecosystem formed is complex. Individual organisms have evolved to exploit individual parts. The system is perfectly balanced:[7] no one part of it can exist without the other parts, the system operates as a whole and can be called holistic. It is this complex system that in some way we need to mimic, taking into account the diversity of human interaction and needs.

THE NATURE OF THE ENVIRONMENT, MIMICKING NATURAL SYSTEMS – THE DEVELOPMENT OF A THEORETICAL CONTEXT

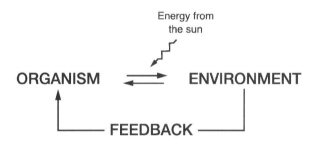

Figure 9.2 The natural relationship between an organism and the environment. In the natural relationship the system is driven by the energy of the sun. Once developed, it is in complete harmony with the environment and is held in check by limiting factors which cause negative feedback and limit the growth of the population. As such the environment remains stable for long periods. Such a system can be described as 'closed' since it maintains itself.

In contrast, Figure 9.3 shows the human condition, developed from a natural system with a stable environment to one where resources have been used and not replenished and which has become unstable. It differs radically from the natural model in that it is a linear system, eating up resources and spewing out waste. The exploitation of these resources has resulted in the removal of the limiting factors – the natural constraints which control the system. For example, the natural limits on food availability have been removed by agricultural improvement. Other limiting factors have been removed by developments in science and technology.

THE CURRENT HUMAN/ENVIRONMENT RELATIONSHIP IN AN INDUSTRIALIZED SOCIETY

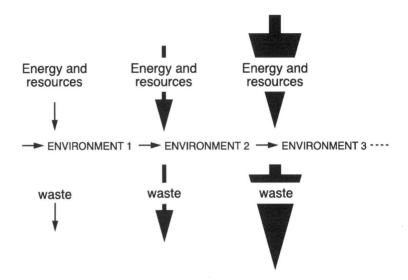

Figure 9.3 The current human/environment relationship in an industrialized society. In contrast to a natural system, humans, through the development of technology and industrialization, have progressively removed the limiting factors, hence there is no feedback mechanism and the system progressively changes, causing environmental change and deterioration. Note that the large energy inputs derived from fossil fuels and use of resources apparently feed in from nowhere as though they are in infinite supply; similarly waste accumulates as if of no consequence. It is easy to see how industrialization has caused major change through this relationship, and that the system is clearly unsustainable.

Unlike the natural system, where the environment remains stable, this system is characterized by environmental change. In this system the greater the anthropogenic influences arising from unnatural processes such as industrialization, the greater the amount and pace of environmental change.

Unlike the natural system, human/environment interaction is ecologically very crude. Energy and resources, particularly from fossil sources, are exploited and waste is produced which is dumped. The more resources are used, the more waste is produced and the system starts to run away with itself, causing severe global pollution. This, in essence, is what is happening now with global warming, the destruction of the ozone layer, acid rain and the pollution of the seas.[1,8,9] This excessive build up of waste is anthropogenic, caused by human activity. The concern is that these effects will become so severe that the environment will no longer be able to sustain current patterns of life.

Figure 9.4 shows the changed relationship developed in a sustainable environment which mimics the natural system. A feedback loop is introduced to constrain the system, keeping it stable. This constraint is environmental concern and manifests itself in social, cultural and political values, including professional values. There is now an attempt to make the environment stable, which means considering carefully the inputs and the use of energy and resources, and reducing the amount of waste produced.

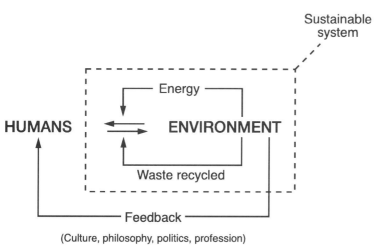

Figure 9.4 Introducing stability into the human/environment relationship. To obtain a sustainable relationship the system has to mimic the stable relationship by introducing negative feedback to control it. This is introduced in the form of environmental concern and consensus on the type of environment we want. The environment is now made stable by choice through political, social and cultural means. The three factors of energy, resources and waste are now properly represented as affecting the system and feeding back into it. The only way to address problems of resource depletion and global pollution arising from these factors is to manipulate them to ensure that problems do not occur. Thus all aspects of environmental interaction become subject to these constraints and a sustainable system is produced through environmental efficiencies.

As with the natural system, there is a need to recycle at all stages to ensure that little is lost. But unlike the natural system (where the energy to sustain the system is derived from the sun), energy and resources are extracted from the environment. Hence in Figure 9.4 the loops which originate from the environment are fed back in by the process of recycling. We set the values for this sustainable system – that is, we decide the type of environment that we want. Thus the left-hand side of the equation is set by human values but the right-hand side is set by our definition of sustainability and our definition of environment and with the energy and waste loops driven by sustainable development. Straight away we see that, as in nature, sustainable development is characterized by careful use of resources and recycling and that, as in nature, there are likely to be many niches of opportunity which need to be identified, exploited and interwoven into the system to refine it. When this is done the system becomes holistic in that each part is interdependent upon its constituent parts.

This theoretical relationship can be considered on a global scale through political discussion concerned with setting values, as, for example, in the Rio Summit.[10] It works equally well on setting policies on a national, regional or local scale for precise pieces of environment.[11] The attitudes of professionals and the professions themselves are clearly critical in determining the outcome. In the current relationship with the environment many of these niches are already present but they are not usually considered in a holistic way. Often they are promoted by individual professions, for example by nature conservationists and energy specialists, but the professions do not always come together. It is important that they should do so.

VALUING THE ENVIRONMENT

Can human interaction with the environment change to improve the environmental quality? In theory, through environmental efficiency, large savings should be possible in both use of resources and waste production. These efficiencies can be realized through the development of holistic ideals, and the identification of the niches of opportunity such as:

- highly refined recycling;
- energy conservation;
- the careful use of materials and multipurpose as opposed to single-purpose land uses.

In considering environmental value it has been assumed, in the past, that the environment can continue to provide indefinite resources, but this is not so since the nature of resources is finite. A deterioration in the environment means a loss, while conversely an improvement in the environment means a gain. Hence it is possible to keep an account which shows environmental accumulation or depreciation.[6] From past development, the environmental balance sheet has accumulated a large deficit as finite resources have been used up and global pollution has proceeded. This was not recognized at the time, but in the future the balance sheet needs to be adjusted to address this deficiency.

To define these terms and to assist further explanation, it is possible to consider the environment and its value under three main headings:

1. As a provider of resources (including energy).
2. As a habitat (including natural habitat and human habitat).
3. As a sink for waste (its ability to recycle waste).

RESOURCES   The term **resources** covers a wide range including free pure water and clean air, land as a resource for growing crops or for the erection of buildings, factories and houses, and land as a reserve of minerals such as rock, aggregates and fossil fuels. Clearly these are finite resources, and their exploitation must proceed with caution.[11]

HABITAT   The term **habitat** is used broadly to define the place where organisms live; hence there are natural habitats, as well as the built environment which forms a manipulated habitat for our own occupation. The human habitat includes the fabric of the urban spaces as well as the countryside, the beaches on the coast and other leisure-time locations. It is our home and is familiar.

Natural habitat is under threat as more and more of the world is developed. The situation is complex since included in our values we consider the presence of other species that we would wish to see thrive.[12]

It is wise to emphasize the point that we are trying to develop sustainability in relation to the manipulated environment. True natural areas of the globe are already sustainable – we have already established this. They simply need to be left alone, or protected by appropriate legislation. It also follows that the closer a system resembles a natural system the more it is likely to be naturally sustainable. For example, a piece of ancient woodland in rural Britain is similar to true native woodland and forms a sustainable system by continuing to exist without any need for inputs, although it provides multipurpose outputs such as landscape, nature conservation, shelter, recreation and timber production.

The loss of environmental quality, in the form of habitat loss or degradation, species loss, or a general deterioration in urban fabric or rural landscapes, all mean environmental depreciation and should be accounted for. In contrast the development of an environment to enhance its character and to make it suitable for a greater range of species, increasing biodiversity, will improve our environmental assets and help to balance our environmental accounts.

WORKPIECE 9.1

RESOURCE AND HABITAT

List as many uses for land as possible. Re-read the sections on resources and habitat and then, following these ideas, divide the uses into two lists:

- Those uses which can be considered under the heading of a 'resource'.
- Those which can be considered under the heading of 'habitat'.

Attempt to optimize the use of the land by putting all compatible uses together. You will probably have a number of conflicting uses left over – how are these to be considered?

WORKPIECE 9.2

NATURAL AND BUILT COMPONENTS OF THE ENVIRONMENT

Imagine the environment in which you would like to live.

List the main features of this environment to define its qualities.

Divide the list into two to give the natural components and the built components.

Finally, consider how the two could and should interact.

SINK FOR WASTE The environment has the capacity to absorb, break down and recycle waste through the natural biological processes. If waste is not naturally broken down it accumulates to such high levels that it becomes toxic. Again the ability of the environment to absorb and recycle waste has previously been thought of as unlimited rather than finite. It is anthropogenic wastes that are of concern – the wastes generated through human development which are accumulating to cause global pollution.

Foremost among these pollutant wastes are the **'greenhouse gases'**, the accumulation of which in the atmosphere is responsible for global warming, and the accumulation of sulphur dioxide that results in acid rain. The table in Figure 9.5 gives the principal anthropogenic gases responsible for global warming. The main generation is through the burning of fossil fuels for energy production.

(a) Gases and their sources

Gas		Principal source	Contribution to global warming %
(i)	Carbon dioxide	Fossil fuel burning deforestation	55%
(ii)	Chlorofluorocarbons	Industrial uses CFCs and related refrigerants and solvents	24%
(iii)	Methane	Rice paddies Enteric fermentation Gas leakage	15%
(iv)	Nitrous oxide	Biomass burning Fertilizer use Fossil fuel burning	6%

(b) Estimate of contribution to global warming by use

Use	Contribution to global warming %
Energy use & production	57%
CFCs	17%
Agriculture	14%
Deforestation	9%
Other industrial	3%

Note: CFCs are entirely artificial gases which are also known to deplete ozone and are being phased out by industry.

Source: Leggett J. 1990. *Global Warming*, Oxford University Press. Other investigators quote similar figures.

Figure 9.5 The common anthropogenic gases which contribute to the 'greenhouse' effect.

ENVIRONMENTAL AUDITS

Can we really place a value on the environment? Using the three environmental valuation factors – provider of resources, habitat and a sink for waste – it is possible to undertake an audit to calculate the value of a piece of environment. In practice this is much more difficult than it sounds because conventional valuation is tied up with the market economy and monetary values, whereas environmental value relies more on subjective values[6] and is bound up with culture, philosophy and politics.

Hence the jostling for acceptance of definitions and action which occurred at the Rio Summit.[10]

Nevertheless, using those three categories it is possible to consider the relative values of a piece of environment which may be a specific site or an entire region or country. In the former case the valuation will affect action (the use and design of the site); in the latter it will identify policy. An audit of the site's present environmental quality set against development options and the potential improvement and possible losses in environmental quality allows a sort of balance sheet to be produced which tests all options.

This qualitative approach is defined by optimizing environmental assets, and considers how this piece of environment can best be utilized. In natural systems, such as a tropical rain forest, the decision should be leave it as it is – for its primary value of species diversity, and as a sink for carbon dioxide, is carefully controlled to keep the system within the constraints of nature. In other areas it should be possible to construct thematic maps which demonstrate the principal environmental value of an area.

WORKPIECE 9.3

ENVIRONMENTAL VALUE

Take the information developed in Workpiece 9.1 and attempt to value the land uses, by giving uses a negative value where development causes a loss in environmental quality and a positive value where the environment is being improved.

As a basis use the idea of environmental equity. You will probably find that there is an overall deterioration in environmental value which has to be addressed by further manipulation to balance your assets and by other as yet unidentified environmental efficiencies.

If you have included energy derived from fossil fuels in your valuation, it is likely that you will have a large environmental deficit which can only be addressed by obtaining energy from other, non-polluting sources.

There are many systems of land classification which place a value on a particular area and which should be considered in developing environmental audit systems. Most, such as the classification of nature conservation sites,[13] rely on a qualitative assessment of primary value. There are secondary and tertiary values; for example, there is no reason why a woodland nature reserve cannot produce a sustainable output of timber, or why an outstanding landscape should not create opportunities for informal recreation.

There are also 'new manufactured' environmental systems being developed that create opportunities for multipurpose use. What are they? How do they work?

CASE STUDY: THE DEVELOPMENT OF A MULTIPUR-
POSE RESOURCE – BIOMASS PLANTATIONS One such
system is the establishment of biomass plantations. **Biomass** is simply
a mass of biological material, in this case wood which can be burnt or
processed in a refined and controlled manner to yield energy. The efficiency with which plants trap and convert sunlight is improved through
technology involving the selection of fast growing species of plants and
their improvement through plant breeding. Favourite species include
willow, poplar and eucalyptus and these are established in large plantations. Although the release of energy through burning gives off carbon
dioxide, a potent greenhouse gas, the system is balanced in that the
plants during growth absorb an equal amount of carbon dioxide, so that
the system is benign.

In the UK the system is commercially viable for local domestic and
farm heating and for electricity generation where development has
focused on willows and poplars. A wider range of species would be
expected in the tropics.

Growing energy is an attractive proposition in that it requires little
technology and is well suited to a local rural economy. It also offers additional multipurpose outputs since it can be used as a disposal site for
treated sewage waste which is absorbed by the trees, or to stabilize land,
as well as producing material for bioengineering.

The material is so versatile that one extensive willow biomass plan-
tation can perform all these functions. It is likely that the real
environmental advantages of these schemes will be realized through
multipurpose use, particularly as an energy source, as well as an environmental system.

As discussed, it is possible to build environments for the future which
will conform to the model of sustainability. The built environment professions need to consider the environment and sustainability and it is
likely that they will have to examine their environmental credentials
and ethics as environmentalism increasingly pervades all aspects of
industry.

This question is easier to address in an industrial manufacturing context
rather than a professional context. The manufacturing industries take
their products apart to undertake an environmental audit of the manufacturing process and carefully analyse the environmental impacts of
each product in a 'cradle to grave' life cycle analysis.[14] The product is

**HOW DOES
SUSTAINABILITY
AFFECT THE
DEVELOPMENT
INDUSTRY?
WHAT ARE THE
IMPLICATIONS?**

investigated in terms of its manufacturing inputs, the resource and energy implications, and the outputs in terms of possible production of pollutants. It is further examined during its operational life regarding levels of energy use, the use to which the product is put and the impact of its use on the environment. Finally the product is examined in respect of its recyclability. Is it easily recycled? What are the energy implications of recycling? Can all the components be retrieved for recycling? Are they all recyclable in some way and does the recycling process itself produce undesirable pollution?

LIFE CYCLE ANALYSIS

Life cycle analysis is one form of environmental audit which attempts to analyse the manufacturing, use and recycling of a product. It can be used to address any associated environmental problems by changing the nature of the product or the components. In doing so the audit identifies opportunities for improvement. Many firms are establishing clear criteria and procedures to produce environmental efficiency in their processes. A similar critical process can be, and needs to be, applied to development or development policies.

It is up to individuals and their respective professions to assess their own environmental credentials, and those of the products which they use, and to react accordingly. In essence we must all be environmentalists now. Since we have to work within the requirements of the environment, we must not only manipulate and build places from our own professional perspectives, but also conform to the rules of sustainability where what is taken out of the environment is also put back so that future generations are not compromised by current activities. For example, it might be preferable to specify the use of a high performance cavity insulation material made of recycled plastic rather than a product which is made of virgin resources.

It might seem that this implies considerable restriction on activities but this is not so, as the following example of the solar village at Bournville should demonstrate.

CASE STUDY: THE SOLAR VILLAGE, BOURNVILLE

The solar village developed by the Bournville Village Trust in Birmingham is the single largest project of its kind in western Europe, comprising nearly 300 dwellings built to a variety of design criteria on seven separate sites. All the dwellings make maximum use of the natural energy of the sun for lighting and heating by incorporating passive solar technology in their design and construction in various degrees and ways.

The showpiece of the village is the demonstration house which, in addition to passive solar features, includes active solar systems (Figure 9.6). These collect the energy of the sun and store or convert it into usable energy for distribution around the dwelling by means of fluids circulated by fans or pumps.

The demonstration house includes a solar heated domestic hot water supply, underfloor and ceiling embedded space heating, a hot air recovery system and photovoltaic solar power generation. These features, which incorporate a monitoring system, are designed to demonstrate a variety of solutions to the challenge of energy saving for dwellings.

According to Tom Greaves (Vice Chairman of the Bournville Village Trust), the demonstration house makes it 'virtually independent of external energy supplies for space heating and domestic hot water and although these features will not be paid for by the energy savings they will provide valuable data and experience which may lead to some of them becoming cost effective in the future'.

Figure 9.6 Highlands Close, Islington, London – solar energy incorporated into housing design and layout. Note the solar panels on the roofs covering an area of 140 m² to supply space and water heating to 15 dwellings. (Photograph courtesy of Dr D. Boyds, University of Central England.)

In the remaining houses the technology used is available to any builders. Since 40% of the UK's energy consumption is used in buildings, the implications for energy savings are clear.

ENVIRONMENTAL COSTS AND BENEFITS

Developing countries may be able to assess their environmental resources in a more considered way than the UK, where land ownership and conventional values hamper full consideration of exploiting alternative energy sources (such as wind, hydro and geothermal power) and in developing agricultural systems which more closely mimic natural forest systems.

THE UK WIND RESOURCE   The wind energy maps in Figure 9.7 show the extent of the wind resource in the UK and define areas where it could be exploited. Since the energy question is one of major importance to a sustainable energy policy, the proper exploitation of this resource could be argued to be the primary use of these identified areas of land[15] although this may be constrained by scenic values.

The example of wind farm development, as a suitable use of a site with a good wind resource, is a useful one in illustrating the balancing of environmental costs and benefits (Figure 9.8). Since the wind farm reduces dependency on electricity generation from fossil fuels its development would increase environmental capital, contributing towards a sustainable approach. This has to be offset by the environmental costs of construction, including the energy and materials used in the building process and the pollution that was caused by producing the materials. However, the carbon dioxide pollution could be offset by extensive tree planting.

These are only short-term drawbacks, whereas the wind generation of electricity is of long-term benefit. Tree planting, consisting of a carefully developed landscape, would help to offset the visual deterioration of the habitat and could also be used to enhance the biodiversity of the site. Inappropriate sites would have already been rejected (e.g. sites important for nature conservation or of outstanding landscape value) since changing them would produce a large environmental deficit. Consequently the eventual result is a site where any environmental deficits have been reduced through appropriate action, and where there is a major accumulation of environmental capital. This is a long-term gain and can be handed down to future generations, i.e. the development is sustainable. In particular, notice how the primary aim is

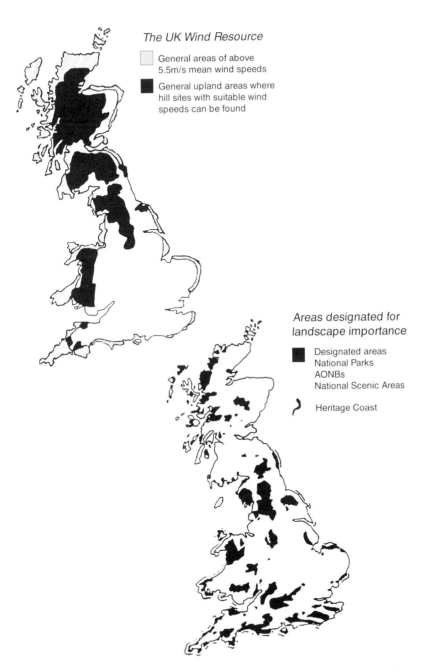

Figure 9.7 The wind resource for the UK compared with the location of areas designated for landscape importance. The use of thematic maps such as these helps to demonstrate the environmental potential or value of the land, where both the wind and the landscape can be considered as natural resources. The problems occur when the different valuations overlap and there has to be a choice. (Source:15)

Figure 9.8 Wind turbine, North Cornwall, UK. An assessment of the UK's wind resources revealed that North Cornwall is a particularly favourable area for the erection of wind farms, seen here developed on agricultural land. In other words the environment has been critically examined and its value as a wind energy source recognized. Similar evaluations need to be carried out to ascertain the primary value and potential of our natural resources.

complemented by subsidiary aims to form a multipurpose system. Several niches of opportunity have been identified to refine the system and make it environmentally more efficient.

INTERDISCIPLINARY WORKING

Similar arguments can be developed in any area, although it is clear that some of the parameters are likely to be beyond the expertise of a single profession – hence the need for interdisciplinary working. For example, there is the potential for interdisciplinary working in the UK local government system, where a range of professionals in a team might include architects, environmental planners, ecologists, foresters, road/transport engineers and building surveyors.

Each profession has its own specific role. Those involved in the more technical aspects of building design need to consider sustainability in the specification and design of materials, in the energy requirements for lighting and heating and in maximizing the efficient use of sunlight for these purposes. Other softer aspects of design and implementation are also involved. For example, the design of appropriate landscapes, as habitat, is an essential part of any holistic system. Existing approaches for the reconstruction of natural habitats are becoming well advanced[16] and there is also a much greater understanding of our possible relationship with the natural environment in urban areas.[15,17,18]

In developing a sustainable approach it may be legitimate to suffer short-term environmental damage for the sake of long-term sustainability which is capable of repairing that damage.[6] This sort of trade-off is advocated as legitimate, but it must mean real gains where the pay-back is obvious and explicit. It is about more than just optimizing environmental quality; it is also about developing sustainable technology for future generations. It is likely that we are at the start of a technological revolution where energy production, energy efficiency, recycling and the design of materials and products are going to vastly outperform their current counterparts. Technology can already drastically improve the efficiency of products.

Take, for example, the treatment of waste. Where once all waste was simply burned or buried in a hole, it is now reused and valued as a resource.

The throwaway society of recent years is being progressively replaced by a recycling mentality, the development of which is a critical part of sustainability philosophy. Waste must be considered as a resource to be recycled and reused as many times as possible to reduce demands for finite resources and ensure the energy conscious use of materials (Figure 9.9).

The environmentally conscious countries of Europe lead the way in recycling. Germany, for example, recycles half its rubbish, while Denmark tops the European league with a need to bury only 12% of its domestic waste.

Waste continues to be recovered and recycled on a commercial scale into a variety of products as methods of recovery become more refined. Product design emphasizes increasingly the use of easily recyclable materials, which can be readily broken down into their component parts. The employment of materials that cannot be reused or are toxic to the environment, such as mercury in batteries, is gradually being reduced.

A DEVELOPMENT INDUSTRY TO SERVE SUSTAINABILITY

HOW CAN WASTE BECOME A RESOURCE?

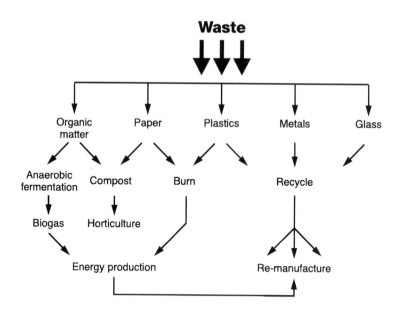

Figure 9.9 Pathways for reusing waste. Note that a variety of individual niches have been identified to reutilize waste, and that waste now becomes a valuable resource – a key part to the development of sustainability. This diagram is of course very simple and each sector could be fully analysed in turn to identify specific opportunities, source of waste and appropriate reuse, developing a far more efficient system.

Recycled materials can show large environmental savings, reduce production costs for industry and provide further incentives to continue to recycle and to increase the range of products that can be made from recycled material.

DEVELOPMENT OF SUSTAINABILITY

It is possible to carry out tests to find the most appropriate use of land or to defend the existing use against change. Through this process the development industry could gradually adopt principles of sustainability. In each of the professions there are elements that clearly promote these ideals; for example, the use of solar heating in building construction, the development of new materials, the exploitation of waste tips to generate methane for energy; more recycling points in urban areas and the development of multipurpose landscape and forestry systems. Each aspect will occupy a niche of opportunity and fit into the overall jigsaw of sustainability to produce a more efficient environmental system.

Our approach to the use of finite resources needs to change by recognizing the processes which underlie the concept of sustainable development. The primary area is energy generation and use, closely followed by the recycling of resources. These have been highlighted as key areas.

In the UK the search for alternative energy sources to replace conventional fossil fuels is headed by the Energy Technology Support Unit (ETSU), funded by the Department of Energy. The department also spearheads the drive to ensure the efficient use of energy, as there is little point in finding alternative sources if energy use is inefficient. It is estimated that 20% of UK energy consumption could be saved by efficient use of energy. Fossil fuels are a finite resource and their use causes global pollution. Alternative sources of energy need to be both renewable and non-polluting (Figure 9.10). The department's research programme is divided into three categories:

ALTERNATIVE ENERGY DEVELOPMENT IN THE UK

- **Economically attractive** technologies are those that are cost effective in some markets and are to make a significant contribution to UK energy supplies before the end of this century.
- **Promising but uncertain** technologies are those likely to become competitive.
- **Long-shot** technologies are those that might be cost effective but only if there are dramatic improvements in costs or if a sharp increase in fuel prices occurs.

It is interesting to note that technology is costed in conventional economic terms and does not appear to include the environmental savings which would be accrued by switching to alternatives.

A different approach, pioneered by the Alternative Energy Centre in mid Wales, is self-sufficiency in energy. The local generation of energy by alternative means is used to supply an individual dwelling or a group of dwellings, in an integrated system of development. This approach may be less suitable for current industrial energy demands or the existing development system in the UK, but may be quite practical for new small-scale industry. This approach would seem to be ideal for countries that require local use and concentrate on small-scale development and self-sufficiency.

Source	Energy	Potential
Solar heat	Passive solar design	Economically attractive
	Active solar	Long shot
	Photovoltaics	Long shot
Biofuels	Combustion of dry wastes	Economically attractive
	Anaerobic digestion, e.g. landfill gases	Economically attractive
Wind power	Wind energy – on land	Promising but uncertain
	Wind energy – off shore	Long shot
Water power	Tidal energy	Promising but uncertain
	Shoreline wave energy	Promising but uncertain
	Offshore wave energy	Long shot
	Hydro power >3m head	Economically attractive
	<3m head	Promising but uncertain
Geothermal	Hot dry rocks	Promising but uncertain
	Aquifers	Long shot

Figure 9.10 Energy potential – Department of Energy classification.

THE NEED TO CREATE NEW PROFESSIONAL ATTITUDES

We could continue to discuss these and many more ideas, but it is more constructive to consider them in relation to our own professions. These ideas provide the means by which each of us can analyse our own personal and professional outlooks. Sustainable development as a basic philosophy lies behind environmentalism. While we may consider ourselves primarily as architects, planners, surveyors or other professionals, we are also environmentalists.

If we aim to design and build environmentally efficient systems, we need to remember that a system which considers only one objective or one output is unlikely to be as efficient as it could be, because there is probably a whole range of other areas that should have been considered. Environmentally we must value proposals in terms of their impact on resources and habitat and how they affect the environment's ability to act as a sink for waste. We must consider the whole life cycle of proposals from concept to use and after-use; we must identify niches of opportunity which will improve the environmental rating of our proposals and produce a sustainable system.

ENVIRONMENTAL AUDIT

Re-examine the earlier workpieces and critically reassess them in the light of the arguments put forward to get a better understanding of the process of environmental audit, the opportunities and the development of sustainable systems.

PROFESSIONALISM AND SUSTAINABILITY

List and examine the primary objectives of your profession.

Test these in relation to sustainability ideals and then identify secondary or tertiary objectives which you can influence through your professional role. Through this process see how your profession can assist in optimizing environmental assets.

SUMMARY

The age of environmentalism is well under way and it brings with it new responsibilities and new attitudes to the way in which we interact with our planet, and how we value and utilize its resources. We have to work out for ourselves our own personal and professional relationships with the environment, to accept that we are all environmentalists now and react accordingly. Clearly inefficient, wasteful and polluting systems are inappropriate for a sustainable relationship, but by examining natural systems we can identify possible models which we need to emulate. These models point the way to the careful use of energy and the careful use of resources. It is imperative to recycle waste for reutilization, and to promote the ideals of sustainability and sustainable development. These new values identify many opportunities to which industry is already reacting. They do not limit the activities of professions; they actually provide greater purpose and responsibilities in the knowledge that we are all looking towards the future. They underline the need for greater collaboration between the professions and within the industry as a whole. The challenges we face reinforce the argument for the continued development of new partnership approaches to the built environment.

CHECKLIST

The issues covered in this chapter are:

- the sustainable approach;
- human interaction with the environment;
- valuing the environment;
- environmental audits;
- how sustainability affects the development industry;
- using the environment to the best advantage of future generations;
- a development industry to serve sustainability;
- the need to create new professional attitudes.

REFERENCES

1. Simmons, I.G. (1989) *Changing the Face of the Earth*, Blackwell.
2. De la Court, T. (1990) *Beyond Brundtland: Green development in the 1990s*, Zed Books Ltd, London.
3. Odum, P.E. (1972) *Ecology*, Holt International.
4. Simmons, I.G. (1986) *Ecology of Natural Resources*, Edward Arnold.
5. Foley, G. (1987) *The Energy Question*, Pelican.
6. Pearce, D. *et al.* (1989) *Blueprint for a Green Economy*, Earthscan, London.
7. Kupchella, C. and Hyland, M. (1989) *Environmental Science*, Allyn and Bacon.
8. Leggett, J. (1990) *Global Warming*, Oxford University Press.
9. Park, C. (1990) *Acid Rain*, Routledge, London.
10. Local Government Management Board (1994) *Earth Summit Rio '92, Supplement N62 Agenda 21, A Guide for Local Authorities in the UK.*
11. Department of the Environment (1993) *Sustainable Development, The UK Strategy. Summary report*, HMSO, London.
12. Evans, D. (1991) *A History of Nature Conservation in Britain*, Routledge.
13. Department of the Environment (1987) *Nature Conservation*, circular 27/87, HMSO, London.
14. Department of the Environment/Department of Trade and Industry (1989) *Environmental Labelling, A Discussion Paper*, HMSO, London.
15. Coles, R.W. and Taylor, J. (1993) Windpower and Planning. *Land Use Policy*, July.
16. Buckley, G.P. (1989) *Biological Habitat Construction*, Belhaven Press.
17. Nicholson Lord, D. (1987) *The Greening of the Cities*, Routledge/Kegan Paul.
18. Gilbert, O.L. (1989) *Ecology of Urban Habitats*, Chapman & Hall.

Allen, E. (1992) *Energy Resources for a Changing World*, Cambridge University Press.

Rosenberg, P. (1992) *The Alternative Energy Handbook*, Prentice Hall.

Toke, D. (1990) *Green Energy*, Greenprint, London.

BIOMASS PLANTATIONS Based on the author's own experience but similar and additional information regarding the UK is obtainable from the Renewable Energy Enquiries Bureau, Energy Technology Support Unit, Harwell, Oxfordshire.

THE SOLAR VILLAGE, BOURNVILLE Taken from publicity material published by the Bournville Village Trust, Oak Tree Lane, Bournville, Birmingham.

ALTERNATIVE ENERGY DEVELOPMENT IN THE UK Taken from material published by the UK Department of Trade and Industry; details available from the Renewable Energy Enquiries Bureau, ETSU, Harwell, Oxfordshire. The Department also publishes the magazine *Review* which features up-to-date information on the development of renewable sources of energy.

**CHAPTER
TEN**

COLLABORATIVE PRACTICE IN THE BUILT ENVIRONMENT

BRIAN RANCE, TOM MUIR AND TONY COLLIER

THEME

Significant changes are taking place in and around the construction and development industry. Many of these pressures derive from the context in which the industry is set: the changing governmental, financial and political context (Chapters 3 and 4), the desire for greater community involvement fostered by central government initiatives (Chapter 8) and the impact of 'environmentalism' and the concept of sustainable development (Chapter 9). These are only some of the pressures that are acting in a highly complex situation, and the list is not exhaustive. We have identified the historical context of the built environment professions and some of the major trends affecting the construction and development industry. In this final chapter we reflect on the nature of change and the constancy of the issues facing society as the basis for advocating greater degrees of interdisciplinary and interprofessional work.

OBJECTIVES

After reading this chapter you should be able to:

● summarize the arguments for evaluating change;

● understand the challenges of a multidisciplinary approach to development;

- present a vision for the future of the construction and development industry;

- understand some of the differences between professional roles in various countries of Europe.

Under significant pressures the nature of the built environment industry itself is changing. New practices and new roles and relationships are being forged. Change in the industry is endemic and possibly the pace of change is accelerating. These changes reflect the challenges that society as a whole faces. There have been fundamental shifts in the organization and management of the development process involving a reduced emphasis on the public sector as a direct provider and the development of new approaches such as design/build methods and project management (Chapters 6 and 7).

In this situation it is not surprising that traditional professional roles are being questioned. Severe tensions exist between professionals in the built environment due to changing definitions of their roles. A major theme of this book is charting the emergence of a new configuration of possible roles within the industry based upon a flexible team approach in collaborative practice. A more collaborative approach, less dominated by rigid professional demarcation, offers a future vision for the construction and development industry, that is, a vision in which the industry can improve its performance.

Whatever systems society creates, there will always be underlying tensions and problems in the way people interact and undertake their daily business. Every generation wishes to identify goals and objectives and the best means of achieving them. However, the means by which they are achieved sometimes fall short of the ideal and inevitably at some point in time become outmoded. This is as true of the development and construction industry as it is of education and training, the nature of the professions and the changing nature of world trade and manufacturing.

Despite this, constancy can be found in underlying ideas and themes; for example, in the balance between the power of the state and the ability of the individual to control his or her own affairs, the need for a healthy profitable economy while closing the gap between rich and poor, the relationship between art and business and so on. These tensions are important. They can exert powerful creative forces or promote conflict and dissatisfaction. As a society we control these tensions largely through the democratic process. How does this affect the development industry? What are the implications for promoting a greater degree of interprofessional activity in our fields of endeavour?

Just like any other facet of society, the built environment has evolved and changed to meet new social, economic, political and technical demands. The emergence of the professions and their development in the immediate post-war period as the context and background for changes which are rapidly taking place now have been discussed. The ways in which the professions are evolving today and the need for greater collaboration between all sections of the development and construction industry have been explored. Indeed much of this book advocates even greater emphasis on interdisciplinary working in the built environment. In presenting the arguments, however, it is important not to lose sight of the following considerations:

● The nature of the world is such that whatever systems are developed in the final years of the twentieth century will themselves need revising, adapting and changing in the next millennium.

● The reasons for creating new approaches to education, training and practice are integrally tied up with more timeless questions about how to operate efficiently in a pluralistic society, how to ensure vested interests do not run counter to creating a healthy and wealthy society, how to minimize conflict and promote quality and so on. These themes are as important now as they will ever be, or have ever been, and are the real reasons for promoting the changes that have been discussed.

WORKPIECE 10.1

CHANGES IN THE INDUSTRY SINCE 1950

Find someone who has recently retired (at the age of 65) from the industry. In discussion with them, list the following:

● The three most important changes in the industry which that person has seen in their lifetime.
● The three features of the industry that have remained constant.

Analyse and discuss these, asking yourself the following questions:

● Why did the changes occur?
● How did people cope with the changes?
● Why did the features that were constant remain unchanged?

As an illustration of how little issues change and the constancy of human endeavour, it is instructive to consider two great artists: Michelangelo and Alexis de Tocqueville.

In Michelangelo's own writings (and there is a selection of material available), there are often references to the problems and difficulties of dealing with clients, specialist trades (particularly marble cutters), the weight of administration which prevents the artist from concentrating on his work and the lack of appreciation by society. The issues he records sound just the same as the problems many professionals cite today and which will never disappear. It is a mistake to think that they will. It is necessary to ensure that the process and systems which operate, which will never be perfect, do not become ends in themselves, but the means to enable people (in this industry the professions, contractors, local government officers, clients, etc.) to work together to fulfil their ideas and aspirations as efficiently as possible and to the highest artistic and ethical standards.

This is why interprofessional working is so important, because it provides the means for excellence. It does not detract from individual specialisms or the need to recognize the particular breadth of skills required for successful building projects to be completed efficiently and on time. Interprofessional working is a means of promoting both common understanding and achievements as well as enhancing specialist contributions.

In the writings of Alexis de Tocqueville, in particular his book *Journeys to England and Ireland*, we find this argument reinforced on a broader social scale. In September 1833, while staying with Lord Radnor in Wiltshire, de Tocqueville is invited by his host, who is a Justice of the Peace, to attend a sitting of the Petty Sessions in Salisbury. Setting aside the crudity of punishment in those days, the cases he records in his writings are hardly any different from what you would find in a magistrate's court today (including straightforward cases of vandalism in which two young people are tried for throwing stones and breaking windows). Taking account of nuances of the language, we could be reading a report of a court session today in almost any part of the world. The challenge the courts faced then, and still do, is what to do to overcome these problems. What are the relevant public order techniques in the late twentieth century to grapple with such difficult issues? It is certain that the same problems will be around in the next millennium. Society will still need to address the issue in whatever is the most appropriate way at the time.

WORKPIECE 10.2

FUTURE CHANGE IN THE INDUSTRY

Using your experience from Workpiece 10.1, identify:

- three facets of your chosen profession or the industry as a whole that are most likely to change in the next 20 years;
- three features that you believe will remain constant.

Discuss them, explaining your reasons for each choice.

THE LIMITATIONS OF TRADITIONAL APPROACHES

Within the development and construction industry there are similar challenges: how to build efficiently while creating buildings and places that people can understand, enjoy and afford; and how to create a lasting heritage to pass on to future generations. One of the dominant concerns of this book, as discussed by each author in turn, is the poverty of traditional approaches in the development and construction industry in solving the problems of society today. It has been suggested that traditional definitions of a specialist professional are full of inner contradictions and problems and that traditional views of how the development process is organized are insufficiently flexible to deal with current circumstances. Basically the message is one that traditional professional demarcations are untenable and new collaborative team work approaches are required involving a partnership between all interested parties.

It is not that new approaches have not been used, as with the growth of project management and various community-based initiatives, but there is not one generally held view of what the new approach should be. The development and construction industry based upon the involvement of many professional groups is highly complex, and traditional views remain extremely resilient and resistant to change. In this context it is suggested that only by promoting a clear vision of the future that a wide variety of people can share will it be possible to create a sufficiently stimulating and integrating force for change.

FUTURE VISION

Of course this vision may depend on national or regional contexts as different countries face different issues. The principal concerns of the UK industry are to do with the fragmentation and divisiveness of the groups operating within it. Japanese contractors have a very much more cohesive framework, and work closely with the banks and other financial institutions. Some of the professions in Germany and France play different roles from those in the UK. Firms in all countries, however, face the same challenge of how to identify work and gain commissions in their own society and internationally.

In the UK any vision must be based on the following premises:

- Traditional views of specialist professions with their inflexible role demarcations should give way to new flexible approaches.
- An interprofessional approach based upon collaborative practice in multidisciplinary teams and creative partnership arrangements should be fostered.
- New methods of organization and management in the development process which respond most effectively to the needs of the client should be promoted.
- The education of young professionals should lay the foundation of this new culture.

Many recent publications[1] have addressed this issue directly and have promoted an interprofessional future for the industry. Bodies such as the Construction Industry Council have advocated a more collaborative approach to the construction process. The Latham Report[2] has proposed a new form of contract to facilitate these developments. The time appears right for a giant leap forward in the way in which the development and construction industry in the UK is organized.

In recent years the emphasis placed by government on how to make this leap has been for the industry and professions to sort things out together. As a result we have seen the creation of new multidisciplinary bodies and a variety of reports (including those identified here) setting out goals and targets for the industry in the next millenium. But can reports and bodies like the Construction Industry Council sort out the problems fast enough? Is there need for greater government intervention in the industry? Will there be an effective UK industry in the next millenium capable of competing with the big Japanese, European and American multinationals? These questions are also explored in Book 2 of this series (*Design, Technology and the Development Process in the Built Environment*). Here we raise them as major questions for our readers. It is the generation of students enjoying these books who will have the real challenge. If today's leaders do not lay the right foundations now for tomorrow's practitioners, it is the next generation that will suffer.

One of the questions we have to ask is why, with new multidisciplinary bodies and the publication of so many reports identifying the need for change, it is taking so long for any real movement to occur. Is it because the whole nature and structure of the profession has become so fragmented and entrenched or are we looking at changes that will, some feel, weaken rather than strengthen performance?

The Latham Report,[2] the latest attempt to identify the problems, is quite clear about the need for change, particularly with regard to the standard form of contract used by the industry. In earlier chapters we have talked about global changes, particularly within the European Union. In the light of increasing European and global trade agreements it is essential to be able to see changes within the international context of the industry and to recognize variations in different countries. Unless we have the knowledge and understanding about the way the industry and the professions work in different parts of the world, it will be increasingly difficult for UK firms to succeed in an increasingly global market.

DEVELOPMENTS IN TRAINING AND EDUCATION

A vision based on the premises we have discussed is helping to create the basis of some exciting educational developments. In the Faculty of the Built Environment at the University of Central England in Birmingham, the emphasis has been on preparing students for this new future. The curriculum has been specifically designed to develop an interprofessional focus for study where students are exposed to the culture of other professional groups and seek a self-critical awareness of the potential and limitations of their chosen discipline. In this way the Faculty aims to prepare students for, and encourage the development of, a multidisciplinary collaborative future for the construction and development industry. The Faculty has developed common teaching programmes across professional disciplines at undergraduate and postgraduate level. Built environment students graduating from UCE will be special in that they will be carefully prepared for this interprofessional future as well as having the necessary specialist expertise.

Research for the CNAA study on interdisciplinarity[3] indicated there were a few universities with joint/collaborative built environment courses. Since then some of these collaborative courses have changed or become defunct and others have been set up. It is interesting to note, however, that movement towards interdisciplinarity has been greatest at the two universities (UCE and Reading) where strategic studies have been carried out on the built environment. Other universities with more limited forms of collaboration in this field include Strathclyde, Cambridge, Sheffield and Bath.

Clearly changes are taking place within the industry, but the extent and speed of such changes are less clear. The amount of change will depend on the nature of the problem or task, the more complex situations requiring a greater degree of change. The evolution of modern practice may be analysed along the scale in Figure 10.1.[4]

Figure 10.1 Scale for analysing evolution of modern practice.

The limitations of traditional specialist professional approaches have been documented in this book and the emergence of collaborative practices has been described. However, the goal of truly interprofessional approaches is rarely, if ever, achieved, and remains a vision for the future. An interprofessional future would involve:

- a loosening of specialist professional monopoly over fields of knowledge and activity and parts of the development process;
- the development and encouragement of a greater amount of collaborative practice, stressing the importance of team work and partnership at all stages of the development process, embracing all its aspects from funding and finance to planning, design and construction, as well as the management, maintenance and trading of the built environment;
- the promotion of interprofessional education and training.

Moreover, as suggested in Figure 10.1, traditional approaches may suffice for relatively simple situations, where the problem or task faced is well understood. For more complex situations, which it is suggested are becoming increasingly commonplace, it is necessary to adopt an interprofessional approach. Thus traditional approaches may continue to have a role in modern practice but the development of collaborative practice is more likely to be an adequate response to the increasing complexity of the development process today. This book has demonstrated the emergence of collaborative practice in many forms and may be seen as an illustration of the above hypothesis.

EUROPEAN PRACTICE

We have touched on some of the questions affecting the industry in different parts of the world but are unable to explore them in any real detail here. It is, however, appropriate to explore the European dimension in more depth, given the important relationships between the countries that comprise the European Union and the fact that the nature of the professions varies from country to country.

In the period after the Renaissance, architecture continued to identify itself with the original concepts of Vitruvius as interpreted by Alberti in *De Re Aedificatoria* (*ca.* 1440) which stated that the architect must be master of the overall design and construction process but should play no part in the practical aspects of building.

This placed architecture clearly in the realms of the liberal and fine arts traditions which, in general, included most of what could be seen as the design and conceptualization skills required in the development/construction industry. Town planning and surveying rarely have a significant identity outside their immediate terms of reference and the term 'architect' is often used in a generic sense for all such skills, also including interior design and landscape. On the other hand, the tradition of the engineer is powerful in Europe and closest to our own system of having distinctive professional bodies.

A good example of how professions evolved in other European countries can be found in France.[5] As already stated, European architecture owes its heritage to the liberal and fine arts tradition and the concept of *le grand dessein* in France is pre-eminent in this tradition.

It was in 1806, with the establishment of the École des Beaux Artes by Napoleon, that the tone and character of the professions was set. By establishing distinctly separate education systems for architects and for engineers, it served to create a widening of the gulf between the technical professions and the fine arts of architecture, both in education and in practice.

In 1940, the Vichy government of France created the *Ordre des architectes* as the statutory registration body which protected the title of architect and also the practice of architecture. This is the body which oversees the profession today and whilst its protection of the title 'architect' seems to have been effective, it has achieved less success in protecting the practice. In 1975 only 30% of the total building work in France involved architects.

Engineering, as indicated above, has quite a different heritage to that of architecture, although its roots are just as old. Engineering was never associated with the arts, either fine or liberal, and was primarily linked to the physical sciences and mathematics. It was never incorporated into a professional body nor did it have a protected title, since anyone can call themselves an engineer in France. Engineers are closely aligned with public service and the education system operates mainly through the École Polytechnique (under the control of the Ministry of Defence) with the École Nationale des Ponts et Chaussées providing the route taken by an élite group of top-class engineers.

A newer system involving civil engineering departments at technical universities is now available. This has catered for the growth in the private sector that has taken place within the last 40 years or so. The majority of engineers in the private sector work for contractors who offer a design/build service. A number of large independent consultancies do exist which offer clients an advisory service on broad aspects of design and in many cases full design services.

In France, there is no independent profession of quantity surveyors which might be compared to that which we have in Britain. The closest which might be identified is the *métreur–vérificateur*, but this is seen as a technician-level skill and the role is rarely linked with the professions of architecture or engineering as part of a professional team. The title is not protected. There are a number of private firms of *métreur–vérificateurs*; they receive most of their commissions from architects, engineers or contractors and only very rarely direct from the client. In 1972, a professional body was established called UNTEC (the National Union of Technicians of Construction Economy) which had as its goal the establishment of the *métreur–vérificateur* as being of equivalent professional rank to the architect and engineer. This new body brought together some of the earlier associations which had been acting for parts of the profession and the whole direction of UNTEC is towards the concept of an eventual integration of skills through all design/build stages.

The town planner, despite a strong tradition dating from Colbert (1619–1683) and Haussmann (1809–1891), has no real separate professional identify in France and such tasks are carried out by architects and engineers, although many of them may have specialized in town planning. Education and training is available at a number of universities and technical institutions. Postgraduate courses in town planning are also available to those possessing diplomas in architecture, engineering, landscape architecture, etc. at a number of other institutions in Paris and the provinces. The profession is still rooted in the tradition of *le grand dessein*, but there are significant moves afoot to break down this physical approach and incorporate a much wider view of the role of planning in the modern city.

In summary, clearly the different history and traditions of each country will be reflected in the evolution and development of its professional institutions. Despite their historic differences, the trend which can be detected in most countries and certainly in France, the subject of this brief case study, is a recognition of the need both to strengthen the competence and skills of their respective professional members and to break down the barriers between them.

The need to provide interprofessional teams with a clear management framework acknowledging the distinct roles of the client, design team professionals and the contractor (in appropriate projects) was seen as a priority by the government in France. In 1975 an act of reform established a system for this and the duties of all members of the construction and development process were set out.

The introduction of government legislation is certainly not the method chosen by all countries to reform their development and construction industry. We have already discussed how in Britain the professions and the industry are being pushed into reforming themselves. Whether or not this proves to be effective remains to be seen. The movement towards a multiprofessional approach is international and developing at a fast pace. Newer countries are joining the already competitive arena for large and complex international projects and few of these are inhibited by the monolithic professional structures that exist in the western countries. In order to continue to be competitive, our structures must become flexible and interactive while retaining all the skills and competencies which are expected at the highest international standards.

WORKPIECE 10.3

WORKING AS A BUILT ENVIRONMENT PROFESSIONAL IN THE YEAR 2020

Using your own personal observations and what you have learned from this book, describe:

- the kind of organization in which you think you will be working in the year 2020;

- the skills that you will need in order to operate effectively within that organization;
- the kind of jobs you will be handling.

Explain your reasons for your views.

SUMMARY

Conflict and tension arise in almost every endeavour: they always have and they always will. The challenge is to channel these powerful forces into creative ends by promoting collaboration and effective team work in the construction and development industry. As we approach the end of the second millennium, we are seeing vast changes taking place at unparalleled rates and across the whole world. In order to prepare ourselves for the twenty-first century and to tackle the complex social and technological issues ahead, built environment professionals need to think carefully about the nature of the industry and the way in which the professions, contractors and others work within it. In order to facilitate our understanding of collaborative practice in the last two millennia, this chapter has traced some of the tensions and conflicts that have occurred in the past as a background for exploring further the basic need to redefine the organization of the development and construction industry today. Although the book as a whole has been primarily about the UK industry, this chapter also looks at professional practice elsewhere and illustrates problems and issues that relate to many countries.

The purposes of the chapter have therefore been to:

- illustrate the way in which conflict and tension can be channelled to greater effect;
- trace some of the problems that all societies have had to deal with;
- identify the origins of the professions in the development and construction industry, illustrating how approaches vary from country to country;
- explore future possibilities for collaboration and team work in the industry as a whole;
- explain with particular reference to the UK the range of professional roles today;
- illustrate the way in which new collaborative interprofessional practices have emerged in the post-war period.

The overall purpose of this book has been to set the scene for the *Built Environment Series of Textbooks*. It has provided an introduction to the nature and organization of the development and construction industry and to the way it is changing in the last decade of the twentith century, and has tried to promote a philosophy of interprofessional collaboration for the future as a theme for the whole series. There are important links between the books in the series. Issues relating to professionalism considered in Chapter 2 are picked up again in Book 3 in a discussion of the respective roles of the professional and manager. The theme of project management considered in Chapter 7 is developed further in both Books 2 and 3. The whole question of the social and political influences in the environment are identified here in Chapter 8 and to some extent in Chapter 9, and form an important thread in Book 2. The series as a whole offers students the opportunity to acquire knowledge, understanding, skills and attitudes needed for the next millennium while reflecting on the nature of change as it is occurring today.

CHECKLIST

The issues covered in this chapter are:

- meeting the challenge: the constancy of change;
- the limitations of traditional approaches;
- future vision;
- developments in training and education;
- conceptualizing current trends;
- European practice;
- built environment professionals in Europe.

REFERENCES

1. Andrews, J. and Derbyshire, Sir A. (1993) *Crossing Boundaries: A Report on the State of Commonality in Education and Training for the Construction Professions*, Construction Industry Council.
2. Latham, Sir M. (1994) *Constructing the Team. Final report of Government/Industry Review of Procurement and Contractual Arrangements in the UK Construction Industry*, HMSO.
3. Collier, A. *et al.* (1991) *Interdisciplinary Studies in the Built Environment*, CNAA, London.
4. Greenwood, R. *et al.* (1979) *In Pursuit of Corporate Rationality: Organisational Developments in the Post-reorganisation Period*, Birmingham University.
5. RICS (1975) *The French Building Tradition*, Royal Institution of Chartered Surveyors, London.

FURTHER READING

Beacock, P.M., Pearson, J.S.D. and Massey, H.P. (1989) *Characteristics of Higher Education for the Construction Professions*, CNAA. London.

Clements, R.J. (ed.) (1963) *Michelangelo – A Self-portrait*, Prentice-Hall Inc., New Jersey, USA.

Foster, Sir C. (1990) *Cons: Restructure to Win* (Memorandum from former Economic Development Council), HMSO.

Richard Lay's Committee (1990) *Requirements of the Profession: A Report to RICS*, RICS, London.

de Tocqueville, Alexis, ed. J.P. Mayer (1958) *Journeys to England and Ireland*, Doubleday (originally published by Yale University Press).

Centre for Strategic Studies in Construction (1989) *Investing in Building*, University of Reading.

INDEX